EAT THAT FROG!

EAT THAT
FROG!

21 Great Ways to
Stop Procrastinating and Get
More Done in Less Time

Brian Tracy

BK

BERRETT-KOEHLER PUBLISHERS, INC.
San Francisco

Berrett-Koehler Publishers, Inc.
235 Montgomery Street, Suite 650
San Francisco, CA 94104-2916
Tel: (415) 288-0260   Fax: (415) 362-2512   www.bkconnection.com

ORDERING INFORMATION

Quantity sales. Special discounts are available on quantity purchases by corporations, associations, and others. For details, contact the "Special Sales Department" at the Berrett-Koehler address above.

Individual sales. Berrett-Koehler publications are available through most bookstores. They can also be ordered direct from Berrett-Koehler: Tel: (800) 929-2929; Fax: (802) 864-7626; www.bkconnection.com

Orders for college textbook/course adoption use. Please contact Berrett-Koehler: Tel: (800) 929-2929; Fax: (802) 864-7626.

Orders by U.S. trade bookstores and wholesalers. Please contact Publishers Group West, 1700 Fourth Street, Berkeley, CA 94710. Tel: (510) 528-1444; Fax (510) 528-3444.

Printed in the United States of America

Library of Congress Cataloging-in-Publication Data
Tracy, Brian.
  Eat that frog!: 21 great ways to stop procrastinating and get more done in less time / by Brian Tracy.
    p. cm.
  ISBN-10: 1-58376-202-7; ISBN-13: 978-1-58376-202-8
  ISBN-10: 1-57675-198-8; ISBN-13: 978-1-57675-198-5 (pbk.)
  1. Procrastination. I. Title.
  BF637.P76 T73 2001
  640'.43—dc21   00-013189

Copyediting and proofreading by PeopleSpeak.
Book design and composition by Beverly Butterfield, Girl of the West Productions.

FIRST EDITION 2001
FIRST PAPERBACK EDITION 2002
09 08 07 06 05   20 19 18 17 16 15 14 13 12

To my remarkable daughter
Catherine, an amazing girl
with a wonderful mind and
an incredible future lying
before her.

Contents

Preface   ix

Introduction: Eat That Frog   1

   1   Set the Table   7

   2   Plan Every Day in Advance   13

   3   Apply the 80/20 Rule to Everything   19

   4   Consider the Consequences   25

   5   Practice the ABCDE Method Continually   31

   6   Focus on Key Result Areas   35

   7   Obey the Law of Forced Efficiency   41

   8   Prepare Thoroughly Before You Begin   47

   9   Do Your Homework   51

  10   Leverage Your Special Talents   57

  11   Identify Your Key Constraints   61

  12   Take It One Oil Barrel at a Time   67

  13   Put the Pressure on Yourself   71

  14   Maximize Your Personal Powers   75

  15   Motivate Yourself into Action   81

16   Practice Creative Procrastination   85

17   Do the Most Difficult Task First   89

18   Slice and Dice the Task   93

19   Create Large Chunks of Time   97

20   Develop a Sense of Urgency   101

21   Single Handle Every Task   105

Conclusion: Putting It All Together   109

Learning Resources of Brian Tracy International   115

Index   121

About the Author   127

Preface

Thank you for picking up this book. I hope these ideas help you as much as they have helped me and thousands of others. In fact, I hope that this book changes your life forever.

There is never enough time to do everything you have to do. You are literally swamped with work and personal responsibilities, projects, stacks of magazines to read, and piles of books you intend to get to one of these days as soon as you get caught up.

But the fact is that you are never going to get caught up. You will never get on top of your tasks. You will never get far enough ahead to be able to get to all those books, magazines, and leisure time activities that you dream of.

And forget about solving your time management problems by becoming more productive. No matter how many personal productivity techniques you master, there will always be more to do than you can ever accomplish in the time you have available to you, no matter how much it is.

You can get control of your time and your life only

by changing the way you think, work, and deal with the never-ending river of responsibilities that flows over you each day. You can get control of your tasks and activities only to the degree that you stop doing some things and start spending more time on the few activities that can really make a difference in your life.

I have studied time management for more than thirty years. I have immersed myself in the works of Peter Drucker, Alex MacKenzie, Alan Lakein, Stephen Covey, and many, many others. I have read hundreds of books and thousands of articles on personal efficiency and effectiveness. This book is the result.

Each time I came across a good idea, I tried it out in my own work and personal life. If it worked, I incorporated it into my talks and seminars and taught it to others.

Galileo once wrote, "You cannot teach a person something he does not already know; you can only bring what he does know to his awareness."

Depending upon your level of knowledge and experience, these ideas may sound familiar. This book will bring them to a higher level of awareness. When you learn these methods and techniques and apply them over and over until they become habits, you will alter the course of your life in a very positive way.

MY OWN STORY

Let me tell you a little about myself and the origins of this book.

I started off in life with few advantages, aside from a curious mind. I did poorly in school and left without graduating. I worked at laboring jobs for several years. My future did not appear promising.

As a young man, I got a job on a tramp freighter and went off to see the world. For eight years, I traveled and worked and then traveled some more, eventually visiting more than eighty countries on five continents.

When I could no longer find a laboring job, I got into sales, knocking on doors, working on straight commission. I struggled from sale to sale until I began looking around me and asking, "Why is it that other people are doing better than I am?"

Then I did something that changed my life. I went up to successful salespeople and asked them what they were doing. And they told me. I did what they advised me to do, and my sales went up. Eventually, I became so successful that I was made a sales manager. As a sales manager, I used the same strategy. I found out what successful managers were doing and then did it myself.

This process of learning and applying what I had learned changed my life. I am still amazed at how simple and obvious it is. Just find out what successful people do and do the same things until you get the same results. Wow! What an idea.

Simply put, some people are doing better than others because they do certain things differently and they do the right things right. Especially, they use their time far, far better than the average person.

Coming from an unsuccessful background, I had developed deep feelings of inferiority and inadequacy. I had fallen into the mental trap of assuming that people who were doing better than me were actually better than me. What I learned was that this was not necessarily true. They were just doing things differently, and what they had learned to do, within reason, I could learn as well.

This was a revelation to me. I was both amazed and excited with this discovery. I still am. I realized that I could change my life and achieve almost any goal I could set for myself if I just found out what others were doing in that area and then did it myself until I got the same results they were getting.

Within one year of starting in sales, I was a top salesman. A year after I was made a manager, I was a vice president in charge of a ninety-five-person sales force in six countries. I was twenty-five years old.

Over the years, I have worked in twenty-two different jobs, started and built several companies, and earned a business degree from a major university. I also learned to speak French, German, and Spanish and have been a speaker, trainer, or consultant for more than 500 companies. I currently give talks and seminars to more than 300,000 people each year, with audiences as large as 20,000 people.

Throughout my career, I have found a simple truth. The ability to concentrate single-mindedly on your most important task, to do it well and to finish it completely, is the key to great success, achievement, respect, status, and happiness in life. This key insight is the heart and soul of this book.

This book is written to show you how to get ahead more rapidly in your career. These pages contain the twenty-one most powerful principles on personal effectiveness I have ever discovered.

These methods, techniques, and strategies are practical, proven, and fast acting. In the interest of time, I do not dwell on the various psychological or emotional explanations for procrastination or poor time management. There are no lengthy departures into theory or research. What you will learn are specific actions you can take immediately to get better, faster results in your work.

Every idea in this book is focused on increasing your overall levels of productivity, performance, and output, on making you more valuable in whatever you do. You can apply many of these ideas to your personal life as well.

Each of these twenty-one methods and techniques is complete in itself; all are necessary. One strategy might be effective in one situation and another might apply to another task. All together, these twenty-one ideas represent a smorgasbord of personal effectiveness techniques that you can use at any time, in any order or sequence that makes sense to you at the moment.

The key to success is action. These principles work to bring about fast, predictable improvements in performance and results. The faster you learn and apply them, the faster you will move ahead in your career—guaranteed.

There will be no limit to what you can accomplish when you learn how to "Eat That Frog!"

BRIAN TRACY
Solana Beach, California
January 2001

Introduction:
Eat That Frog

This is a wonderful time to be alive. There have never been more possibilities and opportunities for you to achieve more of your goals than exist today. As perhaps never before in human history, you are actually drowning in options. In fact, there are so many good things you can do that your ability to decide among them may be the critical determinant of what you accomplish in life.

If you are like most people today, you are overwhelmed with too much to do and too little time. As you struggle to get caught up, new tasks and responsibilities just keep rolling in, like the tides. Because of this, you will never be able to do everything you have to do. You will never be caught up. You will always be behind in some of your tasks and responsibilities, and probably in many of them.

For this reason, and perhaps more than ever before, your ability to select your most important task at each moment, and then to start on that task and get it done both quickly and well, will probably have more of an impact on your success than any other quality or skill you can develop.

An average person who develops the habit of setting clear priorities and getting important tasks completed quickly will run circles around a genius who talks a lot and makes wonderful plans but gets very little done.

It has been said for many years that if the first thing you do each morning is to eat a live frog, you can go through the day with the satisfaction of knowing that that is probably the worst thing that is going to happen to you all day long.

Your "frog" is your biggest, most important task, the one you are most likely to procrastinate on if you don't do something about it now. It is also the one task that can have the greatest positive impact on your life and results at the moment.

It has also been said, "If you have to eat two frogs, eat the ugliest one first."

This is another way of saying that if you have two important tasks before you, start with the biggest, hardest, and most important task first. Discipline yourself to begin immediately and then to persist until the task is complete before you go on to something else.

Think of it as a "test." Treat it like a personal challenge. Resist the temptation to start with the easier task. Continually remind yourself that one of the most important decisions you make each day is your choice of what you will do immediately and what you will do later, if you do it at all.

Here is one final observation: "If you have to eat a live frog, it doesn't pay to sit and look at it for very long."

The key to reaching high levels of performance and productivity is for you to develop the lifelong habit of tackling your major task first thing each morning. You must develop the routine of "eating your frog" before you do anything else and without taking too much time to think about it.

In study after study of men and women who get paid more and promoted faster, the quality of "action orientation" stands out as the most observable and consistent behavior they demonstrate in everything they do. Successful, effective people are those who launch directly into their major tasks and then discipline themselves to work steadily and single-mindedly until those tasks are complete.

In our world, and especially in our business world, you are paid and promoted for getting specific, measurable results. You are paid for making a valuable contribution and, especially, for making the contribution that is expected of you.

"Failure to execute" is one of the biggest problems in organizations today. Many people confuse activity with accomplishment. They talk continually, hold endless meetings, and make wonderful plans, but in

the final analysis, no one does the job and gets the results required.

Fully 95 percent of your success in life and work
will be determined by the kinds of habits that you develop over time. The habit of setting priorities, overcoming procrastination, and getting on with your most
important task is a mental and physical skill. As such,
this habit is learnable through practice and repetition,
over and over again, until it locks into your subconscious mind and becomes a permanent part of your
behavior. Once it becomes a habit, it becomes both
automatic and easy to do.

You are designed mentally and emotionally in
such a way that task completion gives you a positive
feeling. It makes you happy. It makes you feel like a
winner.

Whenever you complete a task of any size or importance, you feel a surge of energy, enthusiasm, and
self-esteem. The more important the completed task,
the happier, more confident, and more powerful you
feel about yourself and your world.

The completion of an important task triggers the
release of endorphins in your brain. These endorphins give you a natural "high." The endorphin rush
that follows successful completion of any task makes
you feel more creative and confident.

Here is one of the most important of the so-called
secrets of success. It is that you can actually develop
a "positive addiction" to endorphins and to the feeling

of enhanced clarity, confidence, and competence that they trigger. When you develop this "addiction," almost without thinking you begin to organize your life in such a way that you are continually starting and completing ever more important tasks and projects. You actually become addicted, in a very positive sense, to success and contribution.

One of the keys to your living a wonderful life, having a successful career, and feeling terrific about yourself is for you to develop the habit of starting and finishing important jobs. At that point, this behavior will take on a power of its own and you'll find it easier to complete important tasks than not to complete them.

You remember the story of the man who stops a musician on a New York street and asks how he can get to Carnegie Hall. The musician replies, "Practice, man, practice."

Practice is the key to mastering any skill. Fortunately, your mind is like a muscle. It grows stronger and more capable with use. With practice, you can learn any behavior or develop any habit that you consider either desirable or necessary.

You need three key qualities to develop the habits of focus and concentration, which are all learnable. They are decision, discipline, and determination.

First, make a decision to develop the habit of task completion. Second, discipline yourself to practice the principles you are about to learn over and over until you master them. And finally, back everything you do with determination until the habit is locked in and becomes a permanent part of your personality.

There is a special way that you can accelerate your progress toward becoming the highly productive, effective, efficient person that you want to be. It consists of your thinking continually about the rewards and benefits of being an action-oriented, fast-moving, focused person. See yourself as the kind of person who gets important jobs done quickly and well on a consistent basis.

Your mental picture of yourself has a powerful effect on your behavior. Visualize yourself as the person you intend to be in the future. Your self-image, the way you see yourself on the inside, largely determines your performance on the outside. As professional speaker Jim Cathcart says, "The person you see is the person you will be."

You have a virtually unlimited capability to learn and develop new skills, habits, and abilities. When you train yourself, through repetition and practice, to overcome procrastination and get your most important tasks completed quickly, you will move yourself onto the fast track in your life and career and step on the accelerator.

Eat That Frog!

Set the Table

There is one quality that one must
possess to win, and that is definiteness
of purpose, the knowledge of what one
wants and a burning desire to achieve it.

—NAPOLEON HILL

BEFORE YOU CAN determine your "frog" and get on
with eating it, you have to decide exactly what you
want to accomplish in each area of your life. *Clarity*
is the most important concept in personal productivity. The number one reason why some people get
more work done faster is because they are absolutely
clear about their goals and objectives and they don't
deviate from them.

The more clear you are about what you want and
what you have to do to achieve it, the easier it is for
you to overcome procrastination, eat your frog, and
get on with the completion of the task.

A major reason for procrastination and lack of motivation is vagueness, confusion, and fuzzy-mindedness

about what you are supposed to do and in what order and for what reason. You must avoid this common condition with all your strength by striving for ever greater clarity in everything you do.

Here is a great rule for success: Think on paper.

Only about 3 percent of adults have clear, written goals. These people accomplish five and ten times as much as people of equal or better education and ability but who, for whatever reason, have never taken the time to write out exactly what it is they want.

There is a powerful formula for setting and achieving goals that you can use for the rest of your life. It consists of seven simple steps. Taking any one of these steps can double and triple your productivity if you are not currently using it. Many graduates of my training programs have increased their incomes dramatically in a matter of a few years, or even a few months, with this simple, seven-step method.

Step number one: **Decide exactly what you want.** Either decide for yourself or sit down with your boss and discuss your goals and objectives until you are crystal clear about what is expected of you and in what order of priority. It is amazing how many people are working away, day after day, on low-value tasks because they have not had this critical discussion with their manager.

Rule: One of the very worst uses of time is to do something very well that need not be done at all.

Stephen Covey says, "Before you begin scrambling up the ladder of success, make sure that it is leaning against the right building."

Step number two: **Write it down.** Think on paper. When you write down your goal, you crystallize it and give it tangible form. You create something that you can touch and see. On the other hand, a goal or objective that is not in writing is merely a wish or a fantasy. It has no energy behind it. Unwritten goals lead to confusion, vagueness, misdirection, and numerous mistakes.

Step number three: **Set a deadline on your goal.** A goal or decision without a deadline has no urgency. It has no real beginning or end. Without a definite deadline accompanied by the assignment or acceptance of specific responsibilities for completion, you will naturally procrastinate and get very little done.

Step number four: **Make a list of everything that you can think of that you are going to have to do to achieve your goal.** As you think of new activities, add them to your list. Keep building your list until it is complete. A list gives you a visual picture of the larger task or objective. It gives you a track to run on. It dramatically increases the likelihood that you will achieve your goal as you have defined it and on schedule.

Step number five: **Organize the list into a plan.** Organize your list by priority and sequence. Take a few minutes to decide what you need to do first and what you can do later. Decide what has to be done before something else and what needs to be done afterward. Even better, lay out your plan visually, in the form of a series of boxes and circles on a sheet of paper. You'll be amazed at how much easier it is to achieve your goal when you break it down into individual tasks.

With a written goal and an organized plan of action, you will be far more productive and efficient than someone who is carrying his goals around in his mind.

Step number six: **Take action on your plan immediately.** Do something. Do anything. An average plan vigorously executed is far better than a brilliant plan on which nothing is done. For you to achieve any kind of success, execution is everything.

Step number seven: **Resolve to do something every single day that moves you toward your major goal.** Build this activity into your daily schedule. Read a specific number of pages on a key subject. Call on a specific number of prospects or customers. Engage in a specific period of physical exercise. Learn a certain number of new words in a foreign language. Never miss a day.

Keep pushing forward. Once you start moving, keep moving. Don't stop. This decision, this discipline alone, can make you one of the most productive and successful people of your generation.

Clear written goals have a wonderful effect on your thinking. They motivate you and galvanize you into action. They stimulate your creativity, release your energy, and help you to overcome procrastination as much as any other factor.

Goals are the fuel in the furnace of achievement. The bigger your goals and the clearer they are, the more excited you become about achieving them. The more you think about your goals, the greater becomes your inner drive and desire to accomplish them.

Think about your goals and review them daily. Every morning when you begin, take action on the most important task you can accomplish to achieve your most important goal at the moment.

EAT THAT FROG!

Take a clean sheet of paper right now and make a list of ten goals you want to accomplish in the next year. Write your goals as though a year has already passed and they are now a reality. Use the present tense, positive, and first person so that they are immediately accepted by your subconscious mind.

For example, you would write. "I earn X number of dollars per year" or "I weigh X number of pounds" or "I drive such and such a car."

Then, go back over your list of ten goals and select the one goal that, if you achieved it, would have the greatest positive impact on your life. Whatever that goal is, write it on a separate sheet of paper, set a deadline, make a plan, take action on your plan, and then do something every single day that moves you toward that goal. This exercise alone could change your life!

Plan Every Day in Advance

Planning is bringing the future

into the present so you can do

something about it now.

—ALAN LAKEIN

YOU HAVE HEARD the old question, "How do you eat an elephant?" The answer, of course, is "One bite at a time!"

How do you eat your biggest, ugliest frog? The same way; you break it down into specific step-by-step activities and then you start on the first one.

Your mind, your ability to think, plan, and decide, is your most powerful tool for overcoming procrastination and increasing your productivity. Your ability to set your goals, plan, and take action on them determines the course of your life. The very act of thinking and planning unlocks your mental powers, triggers your creativity, and increases your mental and physical energies.

Conversely, as Alex MacKenzie wrote, *"Action without planning is the cause of every failure."*

Your ability to plan well, in advance of acting, is a measure of your overall competence. The better the plan you have, the easier it is for you to overcome procrastination, to get started, to eat your frog, and then to keep going.

One of your top goals at work should be for you to get the highest possible return on your investment of mental, emotional, and physical energy. The good news is that every minute spent in planning saves as many as ten minutes in execution. It takes only about ten or twelve minutes for you to plan out your day, but this small investment of time will save you at least two hours (100–120 minutes) in wasted time and diffused effort throughout the day.

You may have heard of the six "P" formula. It says, "Proper Prior Planning Prevents Poor Performance."

When you consider how helpful planning can be in increasing your productivity and performance, it is amazing how few people practice it every single day. And planning is really quite simple to do. All you need is a piece of paper and a pen. The most sophisticated Palm Pilot, computer program, or time planner is based on the same principle: your sitting down and making a list of everything you have to do before you begin.

Always work from a list. When something new comes up, add it to the list before you do it. You can increase your productivity and output by 25 percent or more from the first day that you begin working consistently from a list.

Make your list the night before, at the end of the workday. Move everything that you have not yet accomplished onto your list for the coming day and then add everything that you have to do the next day. When you make your list the night before, your subconscious mind works on your list all night long while you sleep. Often you will wake up with great ideas and insights that you can use to get your job done faster and better than you had initially thought.

The more time you take to make written lists of everything you have to do, in advance, the more effective and efficient you will be.

You need different lists for different purposes. First, you should create a *master list* on which you write down everything you can think of that you want to do sometime in the future. This is the place where you capture every idea that comes to you and every new task or responsibility that comes up. You can sort out the items later.

Second, you should have a *monthly list* that you make up at the end of the month for the month ahead. This may contain items transferred from your master list.

Third, you should have a *weekly list* where you plan your entire week in advance. This is a list that is under construction as you go through the current week.

This discipline of systematic time planning can be very helpful to you. Many people have told me that the habit of taking a couple of hours at the end of each week to plan the coming week has increased their productivity dramatically and changed their lives completely. This technique will work for you as well.

Finally, you should transfer items from your monthly and weekly lists onto your *daily list*. These are the specific activities that you are going to accomplish the following day.

As you work through the day, tick off the items on your list as you complete them. This activity gives you a visual picture of accomplishment. It generates a feeling of success and forward motion. Seeing yourself working progressively through your list motivates and energizes you. It raises your self-esteem and self-respect. Steady, visible progress propels you forward and helps you to overcome procrastination.

When you have a project of any kind, begin by making a list of every step that you will have to complete to finish the project from beginning to end. Organize the project tasks by priority and sequence. Lay them out in front of you on paper or on a computer so that you can see them. Then go to work on one task at a time. You will be amazed at how much you get done in this way.

As you work through your lists, you will feel more and more effective and powerful. You will feel more in control of your life. You will be naturally motivated to do even more. You will think better and more creatively, and you will get more and better insights that enable you to do your work even faster.

As you work steadily through your lists, you will develop a sense of positive forward momentum that will enable you to overcome procrastination. This feeling of progress will give you more energy and keep you going throughout the day.

One of the most important rules of personal effectiveness is the *10/90 Rule*. This rule says that the first 10 percent of time that you spend planning and organizing your work, before you begin, will save you as much as 90 percent of the time in getting the job done once you get started. You only have to try this rule once to prove it to yourself.

When you plan each day in advance, you find it much easier to get going and to keep going. The work goes faster and smoother than ever before. You feel more powerful and competent. You eventually become *unstoppable*.

EAT THAT FROG!

Begin today to plan every day, week, and month in advance. Take a notepad or sheet of paper and make a list of everything you have to do in the next twenty-four hours. Add to your list as new items come up. Make a list of all your projects, the big multi-task jobs that are important to your future.

Lay out each of your major goals, projects, or tasks by *priority*, what is most important, and by *sequence*, what has to be done first, what comes second, and so forth. Start with the end in mind and work backward.

Think on paper! Always work from a list. You'll be amazed at how much more productive you become and how much easier it is to eat your frog.

Apply the
80/20 Rule to
Everything

We always have time enough,

if we will but use it aright.

—Johann Wolfgang von Goethe

THE 80/20 RULE is one of the most helpful of all concepts of time and life management. It is also called the "Pareto Principle" after its founder, the Italian economist Vilfredo Pareto, who first wrote about it in 1895. Pareto noticed that people in his society seemed to divide naturally into what he called the "vital few," the top 20 percent in terms of money and influence, and the "trivial many," the bottom 80 percent.

He later discovered that virtually all economic activity was subject to this Pareto Principle as well. For example, this rule says that 20 percent of your activities will account for 80 percent of your results, 20 percent of your customers will account for 80 percent of your sales, 20 percent of your products or services will account for 80 percent of your profits, 20 percent of your tasks will account for 80 percent of the value of what you do, and so on. This means that if you have a list of ten items to do, two of those items will turn out to be worth as much or more than the other eight items put together.

Here is an interesting discovery. Each of these tasks may take the same amount of time to accomplish. But one or two of those tasks will contribute five or ten times the value of any of the others.

Often, one item on a list of ten tasks that you have to do can be worth more than all the other *nine* items put together. This task is invariably the frog that you should eat first.

Can you guess on which items the average person is most likely to procrastinate? The sad fact is that most people procrastinate on the top 10 or 20 percent of items that are the most valuable and important, the "vital few." They busy themselves instead with the least important 80 percent, the "trivial many" that contribute very little to results.

You often see people who appear to be busy all day long but seem to accomplish very little. This is almost always because they are working on tasks that are of low value while they procrastinate on the one or two activities that could make a real difference to their companies and to their careers.

The most valuable tasks you can do each day are often the hardest and most complex. But the payoff and rewards for completing these tasks efficiently can be tremendous. For this reason, you must adamantly refuse to work on tasks in the bottom 80 percent while you still have tasks in the top 20 percent left to be done.

Before you begin work, always ask yourself, "Is this task in the top 20 percent of my activities or in the bottom 80 percent?"

Rule: Resist the temptation to
clear up small things first.

Remember, whatever you choose to do, over and over, eventually becomes a habit that is hard to break. If you choose to start your day on low-value tasks, you will soon develop the habit of always starting and working on low-value tasks. This is not the kind of habit you want to develop or keep.

The hardest part of any important task is getting started on it in the first place. Once you actually begin work on a valuable task, you seem to be naturally motivated to continue. A part of your mind loves to be busy working on significant tasks that can really make a difference. Your job is to feed this part of your mind continually.

Just *thinking* about starting and finishing an important task motivates you and helps you to overcome procrastination. The fact is that the amount of time required to complete an important job is often the same as the time required to do an unimportant job. The difference is that you get a tremendous feeling of pride and satisfaction from the completion of something valuable and significant. However, when you complete a low-value task, using the same amount of time and energy, you get little or no satisfaction at all.

Time management is really *life* management, *personal* management. It is really taking control of the *sequence of events.* Time management is control over what you do next. And you are always free to choose the task that you will do next. Your ability to choose between the important and the unimportant is the key determinant of your success in life and work.

Effective, productive people discipline themselves to start on the most important task that is before them. They force themselves to eat that frog, whatever it is. As a result, they accomplish vastly more than the average person and are much happier as a result. This should be your way of working as well.

EAT THAT FROG!

Make a list of all the key goals, activities, projects, and responsibilities in your life today. Which of them are, or could be, in the top 10 or 20 percent of tasks that represent, or could represent, 80 or 90 percent of your results?

Resolve today that you are going to spend more and more of your time working in those few areas that can really make a difference in your life and career and less and less time on lower value activities.

Consider the Consequences

Every man has become great,

every successful man has succeeded,

in proportion as he has confined

his powers to one particular channel.

—ORISON SWETT MARDEN

THE MARK OF the superior thinker is his or her ability to accurately predict the consequences of doing or not doing something. The potential consequences of any task or activity are the key determinants of how important it really is to you and to your company. This way of evaluating the significance of a task is how you determine what your next frog really is.

Dr. Edward Banfield of Harvard University, after more than fifty years of research, concluded that "long-time perspective" is the most accurate single predictor of upward social and economic mobility in America. Long-time perspective turns out to be more

important than family background, education, race,
intelligence, connections, or virtually any other single
factor in determining your success in life and at work.

Your attitude toward time, your "time horizon,"
has an enormous impact on your behavior and your
choices. People who take a long view of their lives
and careers always seem to make much better decisions about their time and activities than people who
give very little thought to the future.

Rule: Long-term thinking improves
short-term decision making.

Successful people have a clear future orientation.
They think five, ten, and twenty years out into the future. They analyze their choices and behaviors in the
present to make sure that they are consistent with the
long-term future that they desire.

In your work, having a clear idea of what is really
important to you in the long term makes it much easier for you to make better decisions about your priorities in the short term.

By definition, something that is important has
long-term potential consequences. Something that is
unimportant has few or no long-term potential consequences. Before starting on anything, you should
always ask yourself, *"What are the potential consequences of doing or not doing this task?"*

Rule: Future intent influences and
often determines present actions.

The clearer you are about your future intentions, the greater influence that clarity will have on what you do in the moment. With a clear long-term vision, you are much more capable of evaluating an activity in the present and to ensure that it is consistent with where you truly want to end up.

Successful people are those who are willing to delay gratification and make sacrifices in the short term so that they can enjoy far greater rewards in the long term. Unsuccessful people, on the other hand, think more about short-term pleasure and immediate gratification while giving little thought to the long-term future.

Dennis Waitley, a motivational speaker, says, "Failures do what is *tension relieving* while winners do what is *goal achieving.*" For example, coming into work earlier, reading regularly in your field, taking courses to improve your skills, and focusing on high-value tasks in your work will all combine to have an enormous positive impact on your future. On the other hand, coming into work at the last moment, reading the newspaper, drinking coffee, and socializing with your coworkers may seem fun and enjoyable in the short term, but it inevitably leads to lack of promotion, underachievement, and frustration in the long term.

If a task or activity has great potential positive consequences, make it a top priority and get started on it
immediately. If something can have large potential
negative consequences if it is not done quickly and
well, that should become a top priority as well. Whatever your frog is, resolve to gulp it down first thing.

Motivation requires *motive*. The greater the positive potential impact that an action or behavior of
yours can have on your life, once you define it clearly,
the more motivated you will be to overcome procrastination and get it done quickly.

Keep yourself focused and forward moving by
continually starting and completing those tasks that
can make a major difference to your company and to
your future.

The time is going to pass anyway. The only question is how you use it and where you are going to end
up at the end of the weeks and months that pass. And
where you end up is largely a matter of the amount
of consideration you give to the likely consequences of
your actions in the short term.

Thinking continually about the potential consequences of your choices, decisions, and behaviors is
one of the very best ways to determine your true priorities in your work and personal life.

EAT THAT FROG!

Review your list of tasks, activities, and projects regularly. Continually ask yourself, "Which one project or activity, if I did it in an excellent and timely fashion, would have the greatest positive impact on my life?"

Whatever it is that can help you the most, set it as a goal, make a plan to achieve it, and go to work on your plan immediately. Remember the wonderful words of Goethe, *"Just begin and the mind grows heated; continue, and the task will be completed!"*

Practice the ABCDE Method Continually

The first law of success is
concentration, to bend all the
energies to one point, and to go directly
to that point, looking neither
to the right nor to the left.

—William Mathews

THE MORE THOUGHT you invest in planning and setting priorities before you begin, the more important things you will do and the faster you will get them done once you get started. The more important and valuable the task is to you, the more you will be motivated to overcome procrastination and launch yourself into the job.

The ABCDE Method is a powerful priority-setting technique that you can use every single day. This technique is so simple and effective that it can, all by itself, make you one of the most efficient and effective people in your field.

The power of this technique lies in its simplicity. Here's how it works: You start with a list of everything you have to do for the coming day. Think on paper.

You then place an A, B, C, D, or E before each item on your list before you begin the first task.

An "A" item is defined as something that is very important, something that you *must* do or else face serious consequences. An "A" item might be visiting a key customer or finishing a report for your boss that she needs for an upcoming board meeting. These items are the frogs of your life.

If you have more than one "A" task, you prioritize these tasks by writing A-1, A-2, A-3, and so on in front of each item. Your A-1 task is your biggest, ugliest frog of all.

A "B" item is defined as a task that you *should* do. But it has only mild consequences. These items are the tadpoles of your work life. This means that someone may be unhappy or inconvenienced if you don't do one of these tasks, but it is nowhere as important as an "A" task. Returning an unimportant telephone message or reviewing your e-mail would be a "B" task.

The rule is that you should never do a "B" task when there is an "A" task left undone. You should never be distracted by a tadpole when a big frog is sitting there waiting to be eaten.

A "C" task is defined as something that would be *nice* to do but for which there are no consequences at all, whether you do it or not. "C" tasks include phoning a friend, having coffee or lunch with a coworker, or completing some personal business during work hours. This sort of activity has no affect at all on your work life.

A "D" task is defined as something you can *delegate* to someone else. The rule is that you should delegate everything that anyone else can do so that you can free up more time for the "A" tasks that only you can do.

An "E" task is defined as something that you can *eliminate* altogether and it won't make any real difference. This may be a task that was important at one time but is no longer relevant to yourself or anyone else. Often it is something you continue to do out of habit or because you enjoy it.

After you have applied the ABCDE Method to your list, you will be completely organized and ready to get more important things done faster.

The key to making this ABCDE Method work is for you to now discipline yourself to start immediately on your "A-1" task and then stay at it until it is complete. Use your willpower to get going and stay going on this one job, the most important single task you could possibly be doing. Eat the whole frog and don't stop until it's finished completely.

Your ability to think through and analyze your work list and determine your "A-1" task is the springboard to higher levels of accomplishment and greater self-esteem, self-respect, and personal pride.

When you develop the habit of concentrating on your "A-1," most important, activity—on eating your frog—you will start getting more done than any two or three people around you.

EAT THAT FROG!

Review your work list right now and put an A, B, C, D, or E next to each task or activity. Select your "A-1" job or project and begin working on it immediately. Discipline yourself to do nothing else until this one job is complete.

Practice this ABCDE Method every day and on every work or project list, before you begin work, for the next month. By that time, you will have developed the habit of setting and working on your highest priority tasks and your future will be assured!

Focus On Key Result Areas

When every physical and mental resource is focused, one's power to solve a problem multiplies tremendously.

—NORMAN VINCENT PEALE

"WHY AM I on the payroll?" This is one of the most important questions you ever ask and answer, over and over again, throughout your career.

As it happens, most people are not sure exactly *why* they are on the payroll. But if you are not crystal clear about why you are on the payroll and what results you have been hired to accomplish, it is very hard for you to perform at your best and get paid more and promoted faster.

In its simplest terms, the answer is that you have been hired to get specific *results*. A wage or a salary is a payment for a specific quality and quantity of work that can be combined with the work of others to create a product or service that customers are willing to pay for.

35

Each job can be broken down into about five to seven key result areas, seldom more. These are the results that you absolutely, positively have to get to fulfill your responsibilities and make your maximum contribution to your organization.

Key result areas are similar to the vital functions of the body, such as those indicated by blood pressure, heart rate, respiratory rate, and brain-wave activity. An absence of any one of these vital functions leads to the death of the organism. By the same token, your failure to perform in a critical result area of your work can lead to the end of your job as well.

For example, the key result areas of management are planning, organizing, staffing, delegating, supervising, measuring, and reporting. These are the areas in which a manager must get results to succeed in his or her area of responsibility.

You must have essential knowledge and skills for your job. These demands are constantly changing. You have developed core competencies that make it possible for you to do your job in the first place. But key results are always central to your work and determine your success or failure in your job.

A key result area is something you must achieve to succeed at your job. It is a task area for which you are completely responsible. If you don't do it, it will not be done by someone else. A key result area is an activity that is under your control. It is an output of your work that becomes an input or a contributing factor to the work of others.

The starting point of high performance is for you to first identify the key result areas of your work. Discuss them with your boss. Make a list of your output responsibilities and make sure that the people above you, on the same level as you, and below you are in agreement with it.

For example, for a salesperson, prospecting and opening new accounts is a key result area. This activity is the key to the entire sales process. Closing a sale is another key result area. When the sale is made, it triggers the activities of many other people to produce and deliver the product or service.

For a company owner or key executive, negotiating a bank loan is a key result area. Hiring the right people and delegating effectively are both key result areas. For a secretary or receptionist, typing a letter or answering the phone and transferring the caller quickly and efficiently are defined as key result areas. People's ability to perform these tasks quickly and well largely determines their pay and promotability.

Once you have determined your key result areas, the second step is for you to grade yourself on a scale of one to ten in each of those areas. Where are you strong and where are you weak? Where are you getting excellent results and where are you underperforming?

> Here's the rule: Your weakest key result area
> sets the height at which you can use
> all your other skills and abilities.

This rule says that you could be exceptional in six out of seven key result areas but really poor in the seventh, and your poor performance in the seventh area will hold you back and determine how much you achieve with all your other skills. This weakness will act as a drag on your effectiveness and be a constant source of friction and frustration.

For example, delegating is a key result area for a manager. This skill is the key leverage point that enables a manager to manage, to get results through others. A manager who cannot delegate properly is held back from using all of his or her other skills at their maximum level of effectiveness. Poor delegation skills alone can lead to failure in the job.

One of the major reasons for procrastination and delay in the workplace is that people avoid jobs and activities in the areas where they have performed poorly in the past. Instead of setting a goal and making a plan to improve in a particular area, most people avoid that area altogether, which just makes the situation worse.

The reverse of this is that the *better* you become in a particular skill area, the more motivated you will be to perform that function, the less you will procrastinate, and the more determined you will be to get it finished.

The fact is that everybody has both strengths and weaknesses. Refuse to rationalize, justify, or defend your areas of weakness. Instead, identify them clearly. Set a goal and make a plan to become very good in each of those areas. Just think! You may be only one critical skill away from top performance at your job.

Here is one of the greatest questions you will ever ask and answer: **"What one skill, if I developed and did it in an excellent fashion, would have the greatest positive impact on my career?"**

You should use this question to guide your career for the rest of your life. Look into yourself for the answer. You probably know what it is.

Ask your boss this question. Ask your coworkers. Ask your friends and your family. Whatever the answer is, find out and then go to work to bring up your performance in this area.

The good news is that all business skills are *learnable*. If anyone else is excellent in a particular key result area, this is proof that you can become excellent as well if you decide to.

One of the fastest and best ways to stop procrastinating and get more things done faster is for you to become absolutely excellent in your key result areas. This can be as important as anything else you do in your life or your career.

EAT THAT FROG!

Identify the key result areas of your work. What are they? Write down the key results you have to achieve to do your job in an excellent fashion. Give yourself a grade from one to ten on each one. And then determine the one key skill that, if you did it in an excellent manner, would help you the most in your work.

Take this list to your boss and discuss it with him or her. Invite honest feedback and appraisal. You can only get better when you are open to the constructive inputs of other people. Discuss your results with your staff and coworkers. Talk them over with your spouse.

Make a habit of doing this analysis regularly for the rest of your career. Never stop improving. This decision alone can change your life.

Obey the Law of Forced Efficiency

Concentration, in its truest,
unadulterated form, means the
ability to focus the mind on
one single solitary thing.

—KOMAR

THE LAW OF Forced Efficiency says that "There is never enough time to do everything, but there is always enough time to do the most important thing."

Put another way, you cannot eat every tadpole and frog in the pond, but you can eat the biggest and ugliest one, and that will be enough, at least for the time being.

When you run out of time and the consequences for not completing a key task or project can be really serious, you always seem to find the time to get it done, often at the very last minute. You start early, you stay late, and you drive yourself to complete the job rather than to face the negative consequences that would follow if you didn't complete it within the time limit.

> Rule: There will never be enough time
> to do everything you have to do.

The fact is that the average person today is working at 110 to 130 percent of capacity. And the jobs and responsibilities just keep piling up. All of us have stacks of reading material we still have to go through. One study concluded recently that the average executive has 300–400 hours of reading and projects backlogged at home and at the office.

What this means is that you will *never* be caught up. Get that thought out of your mind. All you can hope for is to be on top of your most important responsibilities. The others will just have to wait.

Many people say that they work better under the pressure of deadlines. Unfortunately, years of research indicate that this is seldom true.

Under the pressure of deadlines, often self-created through procrastination and delay, people suffer greater stress, make more mistakes, and have to redo more tasks than under any other conditions. Often the mistakes that are made when people are working to meet tight deadlines lead to defects and cost overruns that lead to substantial financial losses in the long term. Sometimes a job actually takes much longer to complete when people rush to get the job done at the last minute and then have to redo it.

You can use three questions on a regular basis to keep yourself focused on getting your most important tasks completed on schedule. The first question is, *"What are my highest value activities?"*

Put another way, what are the biggest frogs that you have to eat to make the greatest contribution to your organization? To your family? To your life in general?

This is one of the most important questions you can ask and answer. What are your highest value activities? First, think this through for yourself. Then, ask your boss. Ask your coworkers and subordinates. Ask your friends and family. Like focusing the lens of a camera, you must be crystal clear about your highest value activities before you begin work.

The second question you can ask continually is, *"What can I and only I do that, if done well, will make a real difference?"*

This question comes from Peter Drucker, the management guru. It is one of the best of all questions for achieving personal effectiveness. What can you and only you do that, if done well, can make a real difference?

This refers to something that only you can do. If you don't do it, it won't be done by someone else. But if you do do it, and you do it well, it can really make a difference to your life and your career. What is it? What is your frog in your work?

Every hour of every day, you can ask yourself this question and there will be a specific answer. Your job is to be clear about the answer and then to start and work on this task before anything else.

The third question you can ask is, *"What is the most valuable use of my time right now?"* In other words, "What is my biggest frog of all at this moment?"

This is the core question of time management. Asking it is the key to overcoming procrastination and becoming a highly productive person. Every hour of every day, there is an answer to this question. Your job is to ask yourself the question, over and over again, and to always be working on the answer to it, whatever it is.

Do first things first and second things not at all. As Goethe said, *"The things that matter most must never be at the mercy of the things that matter least."*

The more accurate your answers to these questions, the easier it will be for you to set clear priorities, to overcome procrastination, and to get started on the one activity that represents the most valuable use of your time.

EAT THAT FROG!

Your most powerful thinking tool for success is your ability to discriminate between one priority and another. Take a few minutes each day and sit quietly where you cannot be disturbed. During this time, relax and just think about your work and activities, without stress or pressure.

In almost every case, during this time of solitude, you will receive wonderful insights and ideas that will save you enormous amounts of time when you apply them on the job. Often you will experience break-throughs that will change the direction of your life and work.

Prepare Thoroughly Before You Begin

No matter what the level of your ability,

you have more potential than you can

ever develop in a lifetime.

—James T. McKay

ONE OF THE best ways for you to overcome procrastination and get more things done faster is for you to have everything you need at hand before you begin. When you are fully prepared, you are like a cocked gun or an archer with an arrow pulled back taut in the bow. You just need one small mental push to get started on your highest value tasks.

This is like getting everything ready to prepare a complete meal, such as a big frog. You set out all the ingredients on the counter in front of you and then begin putting the dinner together, one step at a time.

Begin by clearing off your desk or workspace so that you have only one task in front of you. If necessary, put everything on the floor or on the table behind you. Gather all the information, reports, details, papers, and work materials that you will require to complete the job. Have them at hand so you can reach them without getting up or moving much.

Be sure that you have all writing materials, computer disks, access codes, e-mail addresses, and everything else you need to start and continue working until the job is done.

Set up your work area so that it is comfortable, attractive, and conducive to working for long periods. Especially, make sure that you have a comfortable chair that supports your back and allows your feet to sit flat on the floor.

The most productive people take the time to create a work area where they enjoy spending time. The cleaner and neater your work area before you begin, the easier it is for you to get started and keep going.

One of the great techniques for overcoming procrastination (eating frogs) is for you to get everything completely ready to work in advance. When everything is laid out in order and sequence, you feel much more like getting on with the job.

It is amazing how many books never get written, how many degrees never get completed, how many life-changing tasks never get started because people fail to take the first step of preparing everything in advance.

Los Angeles attracts people from all over America who dream of writing a successful movie script and selling it to one of the studios in the area. They move to Los Angeles and work at low-level jobs for years while they dream of writing and selling a popular script.

Recently, the *Los Angeles Times* sent a reporter out onto Wilshire Boulevard to interview passersby. When people came along, he asked them one question: "How is your script coming?" Three out of four passersby replied, "Almost done!"

The sad fact is that "almost done" probably meant "not yet started." Don't let this happen to you.

When you sit down with everything in front of you, ready to go, assume the body language of high performance. Sit up straight, sit forward and away from the back of the chair. Carry yourself as though you were an efficient, effective, high-performing personality. Then, pick up the first item and say to yourself, "Let's get to work!" and plunge in. And once you've started, keep going until the job is finished.

◆

EAT THAT FROG!

Take a good look at your desk or office, both at home and at the office. Ask yourself, "What kind of a person works in an environment like that?"

The cleaner and neater your work environment, the more positive, productive, and confident you feel. Resolve today to clean up your desk and office completely so that you feel effective, efficient, and ready to get going each time you sit down to work.

Do Your Homework

The only certain means of success
is to render more and better service
than is expected of you, no matter
what your task may be.

—OG MANDINO

DOING YOUR HOMEWORK is one of the most important personal productivity principles of all. Learn what you need to learn so that you can do your work in an excellent fashion. The better you become at eating a particular type of frog, the more likely you are to just plunge in and get it done.

A major reason for delay and procrastination is a feeling of inadequacy, lack of confidence, or inability in a key area of the task. Feeling weak or deficient in a single area is enough to discourage you from starting the job at all.

Continually upgrade your skills in your key result areas. Remember, however good you are today, your knowledge and skill are becoming obsolete at a rapid rate. As Pat Riley, the basketball coach, said, "If you're not getting better, you're getting worse."

One of the most helpful of all time management techniques is for you to get *better* at your key tasks. Personal and professional improvement is one of the best time savers there is. The better you are at a key task, the more motivated you are to launch into it. The better you are, the more energy and enthusiasm you have. When you know that you can do a job well, you find it easier to overcome procrastination and get the job done faster and better than under any other circumstances.

One piece of information or one additional skill can make an enormous difference in your ability to do the job well. Identify the most important things you do and then make a plan to continually upgrade your skills in those areas.

Rule: Continuous learning is the minimum requirement for success in any field.

Refuse to allow a weakness or a lack of ability in any area to hold you back. Everything in business is learnable. And what others have learned, you can learn as well.

When I began to write my first book, I was discouraged because I could use only the "hunt-and-peck" method of typing. I soon realized that I had to learn to touch-type if I was ever going to write and rewrite a 300-page book. So I bought a touch-typing program for my computer and practiced for twenty to thirty minutes every day for three months. By the end of that time, I was typing forty to fifty words per minute. With this skill, I have been able to write a dozen books that have now been published all over the world.

The best news is that you can learn whatever skills you need to be more productive and more effective. You can become a touch typist if necessary. You can become an expert with a computer. You can become a terrific negotiator or a super salesperson. You can learn to speak in public. You can learn to write effectively and well. These are all skills you can acquire, as soon as you decide to and make them a priority.

Read in your field for at least one hour every day. Get up a little earlier in the morning and read for thirty to sixty minutes in a book or magazine that contains information that can help you to be more effective and productive at what you do.

Take every course and seminar available on key skills that can help you. Attend the conventions and business meetings of your profession or occupation. Go to the sessions and workshops. Sit up front and take notes. Purchase the audio recordings of the programs. Dedicate yourself to becoming one of the most knowledgeable and competent people in your field.

Finally, listen to audio programs in your car. The average car owner sits behind the wheel 500–1,000 hours each year while driving from place to place. Turn driving time into learning time. You can become one of the smartest, most capable, and highest paid people in your field simply by listening to educational audio programs as you drive around.

The more you learn and know, the more confident and motivated you feel. The better you become, the more capable you will be of doing even more in your field.

The more you learn, the more you can learn. Just as you can build your physical muscles through physical exercise, you can build your mental muscles with mental exercise. And there is no limit to how far or how fast you can advance except for the limits you place on your own imagination.

EAT THAT FROG!

Resolve today to become a "do-it-to-yourself" project. Become a lifelong student of your craft. School is never out for the professional.

What are the key skills that can help you the most to achieve better and faster results? What are the core competencies that you will need to have in the future to lead your field? Whatever they are, set a goal, make a plan, and begin developing and increasing your ability in those areas. Resolve to be the very best at what you do!

Leverage Your
Special Talents

Do your work. Not just your work

and no more, but a little more for

the lavishing's sake—that little more

that is worth all the rest.

—DEAN BRIGGS

YOU ARE REMARKABLE! You have special talents and abilities that make you different from every other person who has ever lived. There are frogs you can eat, or learn to eat, that can make you one of the most important people of your generation.

There are certain things that you can do, or that you can learn to do, that can make you extraordinarily valuable to yourself and to others. Your job is to identify your special areas of uniqueness and then to commit yourself to becoming very, very good in those areas.

Your most valuable asset, in terms of cash flow, is your "earning ability." Your ability to work enables you to bring tens of thousands of dollars into your life every year by simply applying your knowledge and skills to your world. This is your ability to eat specific frogs faster and better than others.

You could lose everything you own—your house, your car, your job, your bank account—but as long as you still had your earning ability, you could make it all back and more besides.

Take stock of your unique talents and abilities on a regular basis. What is it that you do especially well? What are you good at? What do you do easily and well that is difficult for other people? Looking back at your career, what has been most responsible for your success in life and work to date? What have been the most significant frogs you have eaten in the past?

You are designed such that you will most enjoy doing the very things that you can be the very best at. What is it that you enjoy the most about your work? What kind of frogs do you most enjoy eating? The very fact that you enjoy something means that you probably have within yourself the capability to be excellent in that area.

One of your great responsibilities in life is to decide what you really love to do and then to throw your whole heart into doing that special thing very, very well.

Look at the various things you do. What is it that you do that gets you the most compliments and praise from other people? What do you do that positively affects the work and performance of other people more than anything else?

Successful people are invariably those who have taken the time to identify what they do well and most enjoy. They know what they do that really makes a difference in their work, and they then concentrate on that task or area of activity exclusively.

You should always focus your best energies and abilities on starting and completing those key tasks where your unique talents and abilities enable you to do them well and make a significant contribution. You cannot do everything, but you can do those few things in which you excel, the few things that can really make a difference.

EAT THAT FROG!

Continually ask yourself these key questions: "What am I really good at? What do I enjoy the most about my work? What has been most responsible for my success in the past? If I could do any job at all, what job would it be?"

If you won the lottery or otherwise came into an enormous amount of money and you could choose any job or any part of a job to do for the indefinite future, what work would you choose? What sort of preparation would you have to engage in to be able to do that work in an excellent fashion? Whatever your answer, get started today.

Identify Your Key Constraints

Concentrate all your thoughts on
the task at hand. The sun's rays do not
burn until brought to a focus.

—ALEXANDER GRAHAM BELL

WHAT IS HOLDING you back? What sets the speed at which you achieve your goals? What determines how fast you move from where you are to where you want to go? What stops you or holds you back from eating the frogs that can really make a difference? Why aren't you at your goal already?

These are some of the most important questions you will ever ask and answer on your way to achieving high levels of personal productivity and effectiveness. Whatever you have to do, there is always a limiting factor that determines how quickly and well you get it done. Your job is to study the task and identify the *limiting factor* or constraint within it. You must then focus all of your energies on alleviating that single choke point.

In virtually every task, large or small, one factor sets the speed at which you achieve the goal or complete the job. What is it? Concentrate your mental energies on that one key area. This can be the most valuable use of your time and talents.

This factor may be a person whose help or decision you need, a resource that you require, a weakness in some part of the organization, or something else. But the limiting factor is always there and it is always your job to find it.

For example, the purpose of a business is to create and keep customers. By doing this in sufficient quantities, the company makes a profit and continues to grow and flourish.

In every business there is a limiting factor or choke point that determines how quickly and well the company achieves its purpose. It may be the marketing, the level of sales, or the sales force itself. It may be the costs of operation or the methods of production. It may be the level of cash flow or costs. The success of the company may be determined by the competition, the customers, or the current marketplace. One of these factors, more than anything else, determines how quickly the company achieves its goals of growth and profitability. What is it?

The accurate identification of the limiting factor in any process and the focus on that factor can usually bring about more progress in a shorter period of time than any other single activity.

The 80/20 Rule applies to the constraints in your life and in your work. What this means is that 80 percent of the constraints, the factors that are holding you back from achieving your goals, are *internal*. They are within yourself, within your own personal qualities, abilities, habits, disciplines, or competencies. Only 20 percent of the limiting factors are external to you or to your organization.

Your key constraint can be something small and not particularly obvious. Sometimes it requires that you make a list of every step in the process and examine every activity to determine exactly what is holding you back. Sometimes it can be a single negative perception or objection on the part of the customers that is slowing down the entire sales process. Sometimes it is the absence of a single feature that is holding back the growth of sales of a product or service line.

Look into your company honestly. Look within your boss, your coworkers, and members of your staff to see if there is a key weakness that is holding you or the company back, that is acting as a brake on the achievement of your key goals.

In your own life, you must have the honesty to look deeply into yourself for the limiting factor or limiting skill that sets the speed at which you achieve your personal goals.

Successful people always begin the analysis of constraints by asking the question, "What is it *in me* that is holding me back?" They accept complete responsibility and look to themselves for both the cause and cure of their problems.

Keep asking, "What sets the speed at which I get the results I want?" The definition of the constraint determines the strategy that you use to alleviate it. The failure to identify the correct constraint, or the identification of the wrong constraint, can lead you in the wrong direction. You can end up solving the wrong problem.

A major corporation, a client of mine, was experiencing declining sales. The corporation's leaders concluded that the major constraint was the sales force and sales management. They spent an enormous amount of money reorganizing the management and retraining the salespeople.

They later found that the primary reason that sales were down was a mistake made by an accountant who had accidentally priced their products too high relative to their competition in the marketplace. Once the company revamped its pricing, sales went back up and the business returned to profitability.

Behind every constraint or choke point, once it is located and alleviated successfully, you will find another constraint or limiting factor. Whether it is getting to work on time in the morning or building a successful career, there are always limiting factors and bottlenecks that set the speed of your progress. Your job is to find them and to focus your energies on alleviating them as quickly as possible.

Starting off your day with the removal of a key bottleneck or constraint fills you full of energy and personal power. It propels you into following through and completing the job. And there is always a limiting factor. Often a key constraint or limiting factor is the most important frog you could eat at that moment.

EAT THAT FROG!

Identify your most important goal in life today. What is it? What one goal, if you achieved it, would have the greatest positive effect on your life? What one career accomplishment would have the greatest positive impact on your work life?

Once you are clear about your major goal, ask yourself, "What sets the speed at which I accomplish this goal? Why don't I have it already? What is it in me that is holding me back?" Whatever your answers, take action immediately. Do something. Do anything, but get started.

Take It
One Oil Barrel
at a Time

Persons with comparatively moderate
powers will accomplish much if they
apply themselves wholly and
indefatigably to one thing at a time.

—SAMUEL SMILES

THERE IS AN old saying that "By the yard it's hard; but inch by inch, anything's a cinch!"

One of the best ways to overcome procrastination is for you to get your mind off the huge task in front of you and focus on a single action that you can take. One of the best ways to eat a large frog is for you to take it one bite at a time.

Confucius wrote, "A journey of a thousand leagues begins with a single step." This is a great strategy for overcoming procrastination and getting more things done faster.

Many years ago I crossed the heart of the Sahara Desert, the Tanezrouft, deep in modern-day Algeria. By that time, the desert had been abandoned by the French for years and the original refueling stations were empty and shuttered.

The desert was 500 miles across in a single stretch, without water, food, a blade of grass, or even a fly. It was totally flat, like a broad, yellow, sand parking lot that stretched to the horizon in all directions.

More than 1,300 people had perished in the crossing of that stretch of the Sahara in previous years. Often, drifting sands had obliterated the track across the desert and the travelers had gotten lost in the night.

To counter the lack of features in the terrain, the French had marked the track with black, fifty-five-gallon oil drums, five kilometers apart, exactly the distance to the horizon, where the earth curved away as you crossed that flat wasteland.

Because of this, wherever we were in the daytime, we could see two oil barrels, the one we had just passed and the one five kilometers ahead. And that was enough.

All we had to do was to steer toward the next oil barrel. As a result, we were able to cross the biggest desert in the world by simply taking it "one oil barrel at a time."

In the same way, you can accomplish the biggest task in your life by disciplining yourself to take it just one step at a time. Your job is to go as far as you can see. You will then see far enough to go further.

To accomplish a great task, you must step out in faith and have complete confidence that your next step will soon become clear to you. Remember the wonderful advice "Leap—and the net will appear!"

A great life or a great career is built by performing one task at a time, quickly and well, and then going on to the next task.

Financial independence is achieved by saving a little money every single month, year after year. Health and fitness are accomplished by just eating a little less and exercising a little more, day after day and month after month.

You can overcome procrastination and accomplish extraordinary things by just taking the first step, by getting started toward your goal and by then taking it one step, one oil barrel, at a time.

EAT THAT FROG!

Select any goal, task, or project in your life where you have been procrastinating and take just one step toward accomplishing it immediately. Sometimes, all you need to do to get started is to sit down and make a list of all the steps you will need to take to eventually complete the task.

Then, just start and complete one item on the list, and then one more, and so on. You will be amazed at what you eventually accomplish.

Put the Pressure on Yourself

*The first requisite for success is
to apply your physical and mental
energies to one problem incessantly
without growing weary.*

—THOMAS EDISON

THE WORLD IS full of people who are waiting for someone to come along and motivate them to be the kind
of people they wish they could be. The problem is
that no one is coming to the rescue.

These people are waiting for a bus on a street
where no busses pass. As a result, if they don't take
charge of their lives and put the pressure on themselves, they can end up waiting forever. And that is
what most people do.

Only about 2 percent of people can work entirely
without supervision. We call these people "leaders."
This is the kind of person you are meant to be.

Your job is to form the habit of putting the pressure on yourself and not waiting for someone else to come along and do it for you. You must choose your own frogs and then make yourself eat them in their order of importance.

The standards you set for your own work and behavior should be higher than anyone else could set for you. Make it a game with yourself to start a little earlier, work a little harder, and stay a little later. Always look for ways to go the extra mile, to do more than you are paid for.

Your self-esteem, the core of your personality, has been defined by psychologist Nathaniel Brandon as "your reputation with yourself." You build up or pull down your reputation with yourself with everything you do or fail to do. The good news is that you feel terrific about yourself whenever you push yourself to do your best, whenever you go beyond where the average person would normally quit.

Imagine each day that you have just received an emergency message and that you will have to leave town tomorrow for a month. If you had to leave town for a month, what would you absolutely make sure got done before you left? Whatever it is, go to work on that task right now.

Imagine that you just received an all-expenses-paid vacation as a prize, but you will have to leave tomorrow morning on the vacation or it will be given to someone else. What would you be determined to get finished before you left so that you could take that vacation? Whatever it is, start on that one job immediately.

Successful people continually put the pressure on themselves to perform at high levels. Unsuccessful people have to be instructed and supervised and pressured by others.

One of the great ways for you to overcome procrastination is by working as though you had only one day to get all your most important jobs done before you left for a month or went on a vacation. By putting the pressure on yourself, you accomplish more and better tasks, faster than ever before. You become a high-performance, high-achieving personality. You feel terrific about yourself, and bit by bit, you build up the habit of rapid task completion that then goes on to serve you all the days of your life.

EAT THAT FROG!

Set deadlines and subdeadlines on every task and activity. Create your own "forcing system." Raise the bar on yourself and don't let yourself off the hook. Once you've set yourself a deadline, stick to it and even try to beat it.

Write out every step of a major job or project before you begin. Then determine how many minutes and hours you will require to complete each phase. Organize your daily and weekly calendars to create time segments when you work exclusively on these tasks.

Maximize Your Personal Powers

Gather in your resources, rally all

your faculties, marshal all your energies,

focus all your capacities upon mastery

of at least one field of endeavor.

—John Haggai

THE RAW MATERIAL of personal performance and productivity is contained in your physical, mental, and emotional energies. One of the most important requirements for being happy and productive is for you to guard and nurture your energy levels at all times. Your body is like a machine that uses food, water, and rest to generate energy that you then use to accomplish important tasks in your life and work. When you are fully rested, you can get two times, three times, and even five times as much done as when you are tired.

The rule is that your productivity begins to decline after eight or nine hours of work. For this reason, working long hours into the night, although it is sometimes necessary, means that you are usually producing less and less in more and more time. The more tired you get, the worse is your work and the more mistakes you make. At a certain point, like a battery that is run down, you can reach "the wall" and simply be unable to continue.

The fact is that you have specific times during the day when you are at your best. You need to identify these times and discipline yourself to use them on your most important and challenging tasks.

Most people are at their best in the mornings, after a good night's sleep. Some people are better in the afternoons. A few people are most creative and productive in the evenings or late at night.

A major reason for procrastination is fatigue or attempting to start on a task when you are tired. You have no energy or enthusiasm. Like a cold engine in the morning, you can't seem to get yourself started.

Whenever you feel overtired and overwhelmed with too much to do and too little time, stop yourself and just say, "All I can do is all I can do."

Sometimes the very best use of your time is to go home early and go to bed and sleep for ten hours straight. This can completely recharge you and enable you to get two or three times as much work done the following day, and of a far higher quality, than if you had continued working long into the night.

According to many researchers, the average American is not getting enough sleep relative to the amount of work he or she is doing. Millions of Americans are working in a mental fog as the result of working too much and sleeping too little.

One of the smartest things you can do is to turn off the television and get to bed by ten o'clock each night during the week. Sometimes, one extra hour of sleep per night can change your entire life.

Here is a rule for you. Take one full day off every week. During this day, either Saturday or Sunday, absolutely refuse to read, clear correspondence, catch up on things from the office, or do anything else that taxes your brain. Instead, go to a movie, exercise, spend time with your family, go for a walk, or participate in any activity that allows your brain to completely recharge itself. It is true that "a change is as good as a rest."

Take regular vacations each year, both long weekends and one- and two-week breaks to rest and rejuvenate. You are always the most productive after a weekend or a vacation.

Going to bed early five nights a week, sleeping in on the weekends, and taking one full day off each week will assure that you have far more energy. This added energy will enable you to overcome procrastination and get started on your major tasks faster and with greater resolve than you ever could if you were tired.

In addition, to keep your energy levels at their highest, be careful about what you eat. Start the day with a high-protein, low-fat, and low-carbohydrate breakfast. Eat salads with fish or chicken at lunch. Avoid sugar, salt, white-flour products, and desserts. Avoid soft drinks and candy bars or pastries. Feed yourself as you would feed a world-class athlete before a competition because in many respects, that's what you are before starting work each day.

By eating lean and healthy, exercising regularly and getting lots of rest, you'll get more and better work done easier and with greater satisfaction than ever before.

The better you feel when you start work, the less you procrastinate and the more eager you are to get the job done and get on with other tasks. High energy levels are indispensable to higher levels of productivity, more happiness, and greater success in everything you do.

EAT THAT FROG!

Make an analysis of your current energy levels and your daily health habits. Resolve today to improve your levels of health and energy by asking the following questions:

1. What am I doing physically that I should do more of?

2. What am I doing that I should do less of?

3. What am I not doing that I should *start doing* if I want to perform at my best?

4. What am I doing today that affects my health that I should *stop doing* altogether?

Whatever your answers are to these questions, take action today.

Motivate Yourself into Action

It is in the compelling zest of
high adventure and of victory,
and of creative action that man
finds his supreme joys.

—ANTOINE DE SAINT-EXUPERY

TO PERFORM AT your best, you must become your own personal cheerleader. You must develop a routine of coaching yourself and encouraging yourself to play at the top of your game.

Fully 95 percent of your emotions, positive or negative, are determined by how you talk to yourself on a minute-to-minute basis. It is not what happens to you but the way that you interpret the things that are happening to you that determines how you feel. It is your version of events that largely determines whether they motivate or demotivate you, whether they energize or de-energize you.

To keep yourself motivated, you must resolve to become a complete optimist. You must determine to respond positively to the words, actions, and reactions of the people and situations around you. You must refuse to let the unavoidable difficulties and setbacks of daily life affect your mood or emotions.

Your level of self-esteem, how much you like and respect yourself, is central to your levels of motivation and persistence. You should talk to yourself positively all the time to boost your self-esteem. Say things like, "I like myself! I like myself!" over and over until you begin to believe what you say and behave like a person with a high-performance personality.

To keep yourself motivated and to overcome feelings of doubt or fear, continually tell yourself, "I can do it! I can do it!"

When people ask you how you are, always tell them, "I feel terrific!"

No matter how you really feel at the moment or what is happening in your life, resolve to remain cheerful and upbeat. It's been said that you should never share your problems with others because 80 percent of people don't care about your problems anyway, and the other 20 percent are kind of glad that you've got them in the first place.

In study after study, psychologists have determined that "optimism" is the most important quality you can develop for personal and professional success and happiness. It seems that optimists have three special behaviors, all learned through practice and repetition.

First, optimists *look for the good* in every situation. No matter what goes wrong, they always look for something good or beneficial. And not surprisingly, they always seem to find it.

Second, optimists always *seek the valuable lesson in every setback or difficulty.* They believe that, *"difficulties come not to obstruct but to instruct."* They believe that each setback or obstacle contains a valuable lesson they can learn and grow from, and they are determined to find it.

Third, optimists always *look for the solution to every problem.* Instead of blaming or complaining when things go wrong, they become action oriented. They ask questions like, "What's the solution? What can we do now? What's the next step?"

In addition, people who are habitually optimistic, positive, and upbeat think and talk continually about their goals. They think and talk about the future and where they are going rather than the past and where they came from. They are always looking forward rather than backward.

When you continually visualize your goals and ideals and talk to yourself in a positive way, you feel more focused and energized. You feel more confident and creative. You experience a greater sense of control and personal power.

And the more positive and motivated you feel, the more eager you are to get started and the more determined you are to keep going.

EAT THAT FROG!

Control your thoughts. Remember, you become what you think about most of the time. Be sure that you are thinking and talking about the things you want rather than the things you don't want.

Keep your mind positive by accepting complete responsibility for yourself and for everything that happens to you. Refuse to criticize or blame others for anything. Resolve to make progress rather than excuses. Keep your thoughts and your energy focused forward, on the things you can do to improve your life, and let the rest go.

Practice Creative Procrastination

Make time for getting big tasks done
every day. Plan your daily workload
in advance. Single out the relatively
few small jobs that absolutely must be
done immediately in the morning.
Then go directly to the big tasks
and pursue them to completion.

—*BOARDROOM REPORTS*

CREATIVE PROCRASTINATION IS one of the most effective of all personal performance techniques. It can change your life.

The fact is that you can't do everything that you have to do. You have to procrastinate on something! Put off eating smaller or less ugly frogs. Eat the biggest and ugliest frogs before anything else.

The difference between high performers and low performers is largely determined by what they *choose* to procrastinate on. Since you must procrastinate anyway, decide today to procrastinate on low-value activities. Decide to procrastinate, outsource, delegate, and eliminate those activities that don't make much of a contribution to your life in any case. Get rid of the tadpoles and focus on the frogs.

Here is a key point. To set proper priorities, you must set posteriorities as well. A *priority* is something that you do more of and sooner, while a *posteriority* is something that you do less of and later, if at all.

> Rule: You can get your time and your life
> under control only to the degree to which
> you discontinue lower value activities.

One of the most powerful of all words in time management is the word "No!" Say "No" to anything that is not a high-value use of your time and your life. Say it early and say it often. The fact is that you have no spare time. As we say, "Your dance card is full."

For you to do something new, you must complete or stop doing something old. Getting in requires getting out. Picking up means putting down.

Creative procrastination is the act of thoughtfully and deliberately deciding upon the exact things you are not going to do right now, if ever.

Most people engage in *unconscious* procrastination. They procrastinate without thinking about it. As a result, they procrastinate on the big, hard, valuable, important tasks that can have significant long-term consequences in their lives and careers. You must avoid this common tendency at all costs.

Your job is to deliberately procrastinate on tasks that are of low value so that you have more time for tasks that can really make a difference in your life and work.

Continually review your duties and responsibilities to identify time-consuming tasks and activities that you can abandon with no real loss. This is an ongoing responsibility for you that never ends.

For example, a friend of mine, when he was single, was an avid golfer. He liked to golf three or four times a week, three to four hours each time.

Over a period of years, he started a business, got married, and had two children. But he still played golf three or four times a week until he finally realized that his time on the golf course was causing him enormous stress at home and at the office. It was only by abandoning most of his golf games that he could get his life back under control.

Review your activities outside the office to decide which ones are not important. Cut down on television watching and spend the time saved with your family, reading, exercising, or doing something that enhances your life.

Look at your work activities and identify the tasks that you could delegate or eliminate to free up more time for the work that really counts. Begin today to practice creative procrastination, to set posteriorities wherever and whenever you can. This decision alone could change your life.

EAT THAT FROG!

Practice "zero-based thinking" in every part of your life. Ask yourself continually, "If I was not doing this already, knowing what I now know, would I get into it again today?"

Examine each of your personal and work activities and evaluate it based on your situation today. If it is something you would not start up again today, knowing what you now know, it is a prime candidate for abandonment or creative procrastination.

Do the Most Difficult Task First

The longer I live, the more I am certain
that the great difference between men,
between the feeble and the powerful,
between the great and the insignificant,
is energy—invincible determination—
a purpose once fixed, and then
death or victory.

—Sir Thomas Fowell Buxton

ONE OF THE best techniques for overcoming procrastination and getting more things done faster is for you to start work by doing your most difficult task first. This is truly "eating your frog." It is one of the hardest and yet one of the most important of all personal management skills.

You develop this habit by following these steps:

- At the end of your workday, or on the weekend, make a list of everything you have to do the next day.

- Review this list using the ABCDE Method, combined with the 80/20 Rule.

- Select your A-1, most important task, the job that has the most serious potential consequences if you get it done or leave it undone.

- Assemble everything you need to start and finish this job and lay it out, ready for you to start work in the morning.

- Clear your workspace completely so that you have this one, most important task, like a big frog, sitting on your desk waiting for you in the morning.

- Discipline yourself to get up, get ready, and then walk in, sit down, and start on your most difficult task, without interruptions, before you do anything else.

- Do this every day for twenty-one days until it becomes a habit. With this discipline, you will literally double your productivity in less than a month.

Starting first thing in the morning with your biggest and most important task is the opposite of what most people do. This discipline breaks you of the habit of procrastination and puts your future squarely in your own hands.

Starting with your most difficult job, or piece of the job, gives you a jump start on the day. As a result, you'll be more energized and productive from then on.

On the days when you launch immediately into your top job, you will feel better about yourself and your work than on any other day. You will personally feel more powerful, more effective, more in control, and more in charge of your life than at any other time.

Develop the habit of doing the most difficult task first and you'll never look back. You'll become one of the most productive people of your generation.

EAT THAT FROG!

See yourself as a *work in progress*. Dedicate yourself to developing the habits of high productivity by practicing them repeatedly until they become automatic and easy.

One of the most powerful phrases you can learn and apply is, "Just for today!" Don't worry about changing yourself for your whole life. If it sounds like a good idea, do it "just for today."

Say to yourself, "Just for today, I will plan, prepare, and start on my most difficult task before I do anything else." You'll be amazed at the difference this makes in your life.

Slice and Dice the Task

The beginning of a habit is like an invisible thread, but every time we repeat the act we strengthen the strand, add to it another filament, until it becomes a great cable and binds us irrevocably in thought and act.

—Orison Swett Marden

A MAJOR REASON for procrastinating on big, important tasks is that they appear so large and formidable when you first approach them.

One technique that you can use to cut a big task down to size is the "salami slice" method of getting work done. With this method, you lay out the task in detail and then resolve to do just one slice of the job for the time being, like eating a roll of salami, one slice at a time—or like eating a frog, one piece at a time.

Psychologically, you will find it easier to do a single, small piece of a large project than to start on the
whole job. Often, once you have started and completed a single part of the job, you will feel like doing
just one more "slice." Soon, you will find yourself
working through the job one part at a time, and before
you know it, the job will be completed.

An important point to remember is that you have
deep within you an "urge to completion," or what is
often referred to as a "compulsion to closure." This
means that you actually feel happier and more powerful when you start and complete a task of any kind.
You satisfy a deep subconscious need to bring finality
to a job or project. This sense of completion or closure motivates you to start the next task or project
and then to persist toward final completion. This act
of completion triggers the release of endorphins in
your brain that was mentioned earlier.

And the bigger the task you start and complete,
the better and more elated you feel. The bigger the
frog you eat, the greater the surge of personal power
and energy you will experience.

When you start and finish a small piece of a task,
you feel motivated to start and finish another part,
and then another, and so on. Each small step forward
energizes you. You develop an inner drive that motivates you to carry through to completion. This completion gives you the great feeling of happiness and
satisfaction that accompanies any success.

Another technique you can use to get yourself going is called the "Swiss cheese" method of working. You use this technique to get yourself into gear by resolving to punch a hole into the task, like a hole in a block of Swiss cheese.

You *Swiss cheese* a task when you resolve to work for a specific time period on it. This may be as little as five or ten minutes, after which you will stop and do something else. You will take just one bite of your frog and then rest or do something else.

The power of this method is similar to that of the "salami slice" method. Once you start working, you develop a sense of forward momentum and a feeling of accomplishment. You become energized and excited. You feel internally motivated and propelled to keep going until the task is complete.

You should try the "salami slice" or the "Swiss cheese" method on any task that seems overwhelming when you approach it for the first time. You will be amazed at how helpful these techniques are in overcoming procrastination.

I have several friends who have become best-selling authors by simply resolving to write one page, or even one paragraph, per day until the book was completed. And you can do the same.

◆

EAT THAT FROG!

Put these techniques into action immediately. Take a large, complex, multitask job that you've been putting off and either "salami slice" or "Swiss cheese" it to get started.

A common quality of successful, happy people is that they are *action oriented*. When they hear a good idea, they take action on it immediately to see if it can help them. Don't delay. Try it today!

Create Large
Chunks of Time

Nothing can add more power to
your life than concentrating all of your
energies on a limited set of targets.

—Nido Qubein

THE STRATEGY OF creating large chunks of time requires a commitment from you to work at scheduled times on large tasks. Most of the really important work you do requires large chunks of unbroken time to complete. Your ability to create and carve out these blocks of high-value, highly productive time is central to your ability to make a significant contribution to your work and to your life.

Successful salespeople set aside a specific time period each day to phone prospects. Rather than procrastinating or delaying on a task that they don't particularly like, they resolve that they will phone for one solid hour—between 10 and 11 AM, for example—and they then discipline themselves to follow through on their resolutions.

Many business executives set aside a specific time each day to call customers directly to get feedback. Some people allocate specific thirty to sixty-minute time periods each day for exercise. Many people read great books fifteen minutes each night before retiring. In this way, over time, they eventually read dozens of the best books ever written.

The key to the success of this method of working in specific time segments is for you to plan your day in advance and specifically schedule a fixed time period for a particular activity or task.

You make work appointments with yourself and then discipline yourself to keep them. You set aside thirty, sixty, and ninety-minute time segments that you use to work on and complete important tasks.

Many highly productive people schedule specific activities in preplanned time slots all day long. These people build their work lives around accomplishing key tasks one at a time. As a result, they become more and more productive and eventually produce two times, three times, and five times as much as the average person.

A time planner, broken down by day, hour, and minute, organized in advance, can be one of the most powerful personal-productivity tools of all. It enables you to see where you can consolidate and create blocks of time for concentrated work.

During this working time, you turn off the telephone, eliminate all distractions, and work nonstop.

One of the best work habits of all is for you to get up early and work at home in the morning for several hours. You can get three times as much work done at home without interruptions as you ever could in a busy office where you are surrounded by people and bombarded by phone calls.

When you fly on business, you can create your office in the air by planning your work thoroughly before you depart. When the plane takes off, you can work nonstop for the entire flight. You will be amazed at how much work you can go through when you work steadily in an airplane, without interruptions.

One of the keys to high levels of performance and productivity is for you to make every minute count. Use travel and transition time, what are often called "gifts of time," to complete small chunks of larger tasks.

Remember, the pyramids were built one block at a time. A great life and a great career is built one task, and often, one part of a task, at a time. Your job in time management is to deliberately and creatively organize the concentrated time periods you need to get your key jobs done well and on schedule.

EAT THAT FROG!

Think continually of different ways that you can save, schedule, and consolidate large chunks of time. Use this time to work on important tasks with the most significant long-term consequences.

Make every minute count. Work steadily and continuously without diversion or distraction by planning and preparing your work in advance. Most of all, keep focused on the most important results for which you are responsible.

Develop a Sense of Urgency

Do not wait; the time will never
be "just right." Start where you stand,
and work with whatever tools you may
have at your command, and better tools
will be found as you go along.

—NAPOLEON HILL

PERHAPS THE MOST outwardly identifiable quality of a high-performing man or woman is "action orientation."

Highly productive people take the time to think, plan, and set priorities. They then launch quickly and strongly toward their goals and objectives. They work steadily, smoothly, and continuously and seem to go through enormous amounts of work in the same time period that the average person spends socializing, wasting time, and working on low-value activities.

When you work on high-value tasks at a high and continuous level of activity, you can actually enter into an amazing mental state called "flow." Almost everyone has experienced this at some time. Really successful people are those who get themselves into this state far more often than the average.

In the state of flow, which is the highest human state of performance and productivity, something almost miraculous happens to your mind and emotions.

You feel elated and clear. Everything you do seems effortless and accurate. You feel happy and energized. You experience a tremendous sense of calm and personal effectiveness.

In the state of flow, identified and talked about over the centuries, you actually function on a higher plane of clarity, creativity, and competence. You are more sensitive and aware. Your insight and intuition function with incredible precision. You see the interconnectedness of people and circumstances around you. You often come up with brilliant ideas and insights that enable you to move ahead even more rapidly.

One of the ways you can trigger this state of flow is by developing a "sense of urgency." This is an inner drive and desire to get on with a job quickly and get it done fast. This inner drive is an impatience that motivates you to get going and to keep going. A sense of urgency feels very much like racing against yourself.

With this ingrained sense of urgency, you develop a "bias for action." You take action rather than talking continually about what you are going to do. You focus on specific steps you can take immediately. You concentrate on the things you can do right now to get the results you want and achieve the goals you desire.

A fast tempo seems to go hand in hand with all great success. Developing this tempo requires that you start moving and keep moving at a steady rate.

When you become an action-oriented person, you activate the "Momentum Principle" of success. This principle says that although it may take tremendous amounts of energy to overcome inertia and get going initially, it then takes far less energy to keep going.

The good news is that the faster you move, the more energy you have. The faster you move, the more you get done and the more effective you feel. The faster you move, the more experience you get and the more you learn. The faster you move, the more competent and capable you become at your work.

A sense of urgency shifts you automatically onto the fast track in your career. The faster you work and the more you get done, the higher will be your levels of self-esteem, self-respect, and personal pride.

One of the simplest and yet most powerful ways to get yourself started is to repeat the words "Do it now! Do it now! Do it now!" over and over to yourself.

If you feel yourself slowing or becoming distracted by conversations or low-value activities, repeat to yourself the words "Back to work! Back to work! Back to work!" over and over.

In the final analysis, nothing will help you more in your career than for you to get the reputation for being the kind of person who gets important work done quickly and well. This reputation will make you one of the most valuable and respected people in your field.

EAT THAT FROG!

Resolve today to develop a sense of urgency in everything you do. Select one area where you have a tendency to procrastinate and make a decision to develop the habit of fast action in that area.

When you see an opportunity or a problem, take action immediately. When you are given a task or responsibility, do it quickly and report back fast. Move rapidly in every important area of your life. You will be amazed at how much better you feel and how much more you get done.

Single Handle
Every Task

And herein lies the secret of true power.
Learn, by constant practice, how to
husband your resources, and
concentrate them, at any given
moment, upon a given point.

—JAMES ALLEN

EAT THAT FROG! Every bit of planning, prioritizing, and organizing comes down to this simple concept.

Your ability to select your most important task, to begin it, and then to concentrate on it single-mindedly until it is complete is the key to high levels of performance and personal productivity.

Every great achievement of humankind has been preceded by a long period of hard, concentrated work until the job was done.

Single handling requires that once you begin a task, you keep working at it, without diversion or distraction, until the job is 100 percent complete. You keep urging yourself onward by repeating the words "Back to work!" over and over whenever you are tempted to stop or do something else.

By concentrating single-mindedly on your most important task, you can reduce the time required to complete it by 50 percent or more.

It has been estimated that the tendency to start and stop a task, to pick it up, put it down, and come back to it, can increase the time necessary to complete the task by as much as 500 percent.

Each time you return to the task, you have to familiarize yourself with where you were when you stopped and what you still have to do. You have to overcome inertia and get yourself going again. You have to develop momentum and get into a productive work rhythm.

But when you prepare thoroughly and then begin, refusing to stop or turn aside until the job is done, you develop energy, enthusiasm, and motivation. You get better and better and more productive. You work faster and more effectively.

The truth is that once you have decided on your number one task, anything else that you do other than that is a relative waste of time. Any other activity is just not as valuable or as important as this job, based on your own priorities.

The more you discipline yourself to working non-stop on a single task, the more you move forward along the "Efficiency Curve." You get more and more high quality work done in less and less time.

Each time you stop working, however, you break this cycle and move backward on the curve to where every part of the task is more difficult and time consuming.

Elbert Hubbard defined self-discipline as "The ability to make yourself do what you should do, when you should do it, whether you feel like it or not."

In the final analysis, success in any area requires tons of discipline. Self-discipline, self-mastery, and self-control are the basic building blocks of character and high performance.

Starting a high-priority task and persisting with that task until it is 100 percent complete is the true test of your character, your willpower, and your resolve.

Persistence is actually self-discipline in action. The good news is that the more you discipline yourself to persist on a major task, the more you like and respect yourself, and the higher is your self-esteem. And the more you like and respect yourself, the easier it is for you to discipline yourself to persist even more.

By focusing clearly on your most valuable task and concentrating single-mindedly until it is 100 percent complete, you actually shape and mold your own character. You become a superior person.

You become a stronger, more competent, more confident, and happier person. You feel more powerful and productive.

You eventually feel capable of setting and achieving any goal. You become the master of your own destiny. You place yourself on an ascending spiral of personal effectiveness on which your future is absolutely guaranteed.

And the key to all of this is for you to determine the most valuable and important thing you could possibly do at every single moment and then "Eat That Frog!"

EAT THAT FROG!

Take action! Resolve today to select the most important task or project that you could complete and then launch into it immediately.

Once you start your most important task, discipline yourself to persevere without diversion or distraction until it is 100 percent complete. See it as a "test" to determine whether you are the kind of person who can make a decision to complete something and then carry it out. Once you begin, refuse to stop until the job is finished.

Conclusion:
Putting It All Together

The key to happiness, satisfaction, great success, and a wonderful feeling of personal power and effectiveness is for you to develop the habit of eating your frog first thing every day when you start work.

Fortunately, this is a learnable skill that you can acquire through repetition. And when you develop the habit of starting on your most important task, before anything else, your success is assured.

Here is a summary of the twenty-one great ways to stop procrastinating and get more things done faster. Review these rules and principles regularly until they become firmly ingrained in your thinking and actions and your future will be guaranteed.

1. **Set the table:** Decide exactly what you want. Clarity is essential. Write out your goals and objectives before you begin.

2. **Plan every day in advance:** Think on paper. Every minute you spend in planning can save you five or ten minutes in execution.

3. **Apply the 80/20 Rule to everything:** Twenty percent of your activities will account for 80 percent of your results. Always concentrate your efforts on that top 20 percent.

4. **Consider the consequences:** Your most important tasks and priorities are those that can have the most serious consequences, positive or negative, on your life or work. Focus on these above all else.

5. **Practice the ABCDE Method continually:** Before you begin work on a list of tasks, take a few moments to organize them by value and priority so you can be sure of working on your most important activities.

6. **Focus on key result areas:** Identify and determine those results that you absolutely, positively have to get to do your job well, and work on them all day long.

7. **Obey the Law of Forced Efficiency:** There is never enough time to do everything, but there is always enough time to do the most important things. What are they?

8. **Prepare thoroughly before you begin:** Proper prior preparation prevents poor performance.

9. **Do your homework:** The more knowledgeable and skilled you become at your key tasks, the

faster you start them and the sooner you get them done.

10. **Leverage your special talents:** Determine exactly what it is that you are very good at doing, or could be very good at, and throw your whole heart into doing those specific things very, very well.

11. **Identify your key constraints:** Determine the bottlenecks or choke points, internally or externally, that set the speed at which you achieve your most important goals, and focus on alleviating them.

12. **Take it one oil barrel at a time:** You can accomplish the biggest and most complicated job if you just complete it one step at a time.

13. **Put the pressure on yourself:** Imagine that you have to leave town for a month and work as if you had to get all your major tasks completed before you left.

14. **Maximize your personal powers:** Identify your periods of highest mental and physical energy each day and structure your most important and demanding tasks around these times. Get lots of rest so you can perform at your best.

15. **Motivate yourself into action:** Be your own cheerleader. Look for the good in every situation.

Focus on the solution rather than the problem. Always be optimistic and constructive.

16. **Practice creative procrastination:** Since you can't do everything, you must learn to deliberately put off those tasks that are of low value so that you have enough time to do the few things that really count.

17. **Do the most difficult task first:** Begin each day with your most difficult task, the one task that can make the greatest contribution to yourself and your work, and resolve to stay at it until it is complete.

18. **Slice and dice the task:** Break large, complex tasks down into bite-sized pieces and then just do one small part of the task to get started.

19. **Create large chunks of time:** Organize your days around large blocks of time where you can concentrate for extended periods on your most important tasks.

20. **Develop a sense of urgency:** Make a habit of moving fast on your key tasks. Become known as a person who does things quickly and well.

21. **Single handle every task:** Set clear priorities, start immediately on your most important task, and then work without stopping until the job is 100 percent complete. This is the real key to

high performance and maximum personal productivity.

Make a decision to practice these principles every day until they become second nature to you. With these habits of personal management as a permanent part of your personality, your future will be unlimited.

Just do it! Eat that frog.

Learning Resources of
Brian Tracy International
Double Your Income,
Double Your Time Off

BRIAN TRACY'S PERSONAL COACHING PROGRAMS – THE KEYS TO MAKING A QUANTUM LEAP IN YOUR LIFE AND CAREER
Focal Point Advanced Coaching and
Mentoring Program

Brian Tracy offers a personal coaching program in San Diego for successful entrepreneurs, self-employed professionals, and top salespeople. Participants learn how to apply the Focal Point Process to every part of their work and personal lives.

Participants learn a step-by-step process of personal strategic planning that enables them to take complete control of their time and their lives. Over the course of the program, participants meet with Brian Tracy one full day every three months. During these sessions, they learn how to double their income and double their time off.

They identify the things they enjoy doing the most and learn how to become better in their most profitable activities. Participants learn how to delegate, downsize, eliminate, and get rid of all the tasks they neither enjoy nor benefit from. They learn how to identify their special talents and how to use leverage and concentration to move to the top of their fields.

Focal Point Personal Telephone Coaching Program
Brian Tracy's personally trained professional coaches work with you step-by-step to help you move to the next level of performance in your career.

This intensive 12 week program comes complete with exercises, audio programs, pre-work and personalized coaching.

You learn how to implement the Focal Point Process in every area of your life. Working with a trusted mentor, you develop complete clarity about who you are, what you want, where you are going, and the fastest ways to achieve all your goals.

For more information on the Live or Telephone Coaching and Mentoring Programs offered by Brian Tracy, visit **http//:www.briantracy.com**, call **858-481-2977**, or write to Brian Tracy International, 462 Stevens Avenue, Suite 202, Solana Beach, CA 92075.

Visit Brian Tracy at **www.21successsecrets.com** for a *free copy* of his new audio program, "The 21 Success Secrets of Self-Made Millionaires." You pay only shipping and handling.

Also, check out Brian Tracy's newest books, *Eat That Frog!* and *The 100 Absolutely Unbreakable Laws of Business Success* at your local bookstore or at **www.briantracy.com**.

BRIAN TRACY
SPEAKER, TRAINER, SEMINAR LEADER

Brian Tracy is one of the top professional speakers in the world, addressing more than 300,000 people each year throughout the United States, Europe, Asia, and Australia.

Brian's keynote speeches, talks, and seminars are described as "inspiring, entertaining, informative, and motivational." His audiences include Fortune 500 companies and every size of business and association.

Call today for full information on booking Brian to speak at your next meeting or conference.

21st Century Thinking—How to outthink, outplan, and outstrategize your competition and get superior results in a turbulent, fast-changing business environment.

Advanced Selling Strategies—How to outthink, outperform, and outsell your competition using the most advanced strategies and tactics known to modern selling.

The Psychology of Success—How the top people think and act in every area of personal and business life. Countless practical, proven methods and strategies for peak performance.

Leadership in the New Millennium—How to apply the most powerful leadership principles ever discovered to manage, motivate, and get better results, faster than ever before.

Brian will carefully customize his talk for you and for your needs. Visit Brian Tracy International at www.briantracy.com for more information or call **858/481-2977** today for a free promotional package.

BRIAN TRACY AUDIO LEARNING
PROGRAMS

	AUDIO	CD
❖ **Psychology of Achievement** (7 hours) The most popular program on success and achievement in the world.	$65.00	$70.00
❖ **Psychology of Success** (7 hours) The 10 principles of peak performance practiced by all high achievers.	$65.00	$70.00
❖ **Psychology of Selling** (7 hours) The most powerful, practical, professional selling program in the world today.	$75.00	$80.00
❖ **How to Master Your Time** (7 hours) More than 500 key ideas for time management in a proven system that brings about immediate results. Save 2 hours every day.	$65.00	$70.00
❖ **Million-Dollar Habits** (7 hours) The specific habits and behaviors practiced by high earners and self-made millionaires. Double and triple your income.	$65.00	$70.00
❖ **How Leaders Lead** (7 hours) With Ken Blanchard. How to manage, motivate, inspire, and lead a winning team.	$65.00	
❖ **Advanced Selling Techniques** (7 hours) The most complete advanced selling program for top professionals in the world.	$75.00	$80.00
❖ **Master Strategies for High Achievement** (7 hours) More than 150 of the key strategies practiced by the most successful people--in every area of life.	$65.00	$70.00

	AUDIO	CD
❖ **Accelerated Learning Techniques** (7 hours) How to learn faster, remember more, unlock the power of your mind for maximum performance.	$65.00	$70.00
❖ **Thinking Big** (7 hours) How to dream big dreams, build self-confidence, set goals, develop the mind-set of successful people.	$65.00	$70.00
❖ **The Luck Factor** (7 hours) More than 60 proven strategies to increase the likelihood that you will be the right person at the right place at the right time.	$65.00	$70.00
❖ **Breaking the Success Barrier** (7 hours) The 12 most powerful thinking tools ever discovered enable you to overcome any obstacle, achieve any goal.	$65.00	$70.00

❖ SPECIAL OFFER ❖

Any 1 program—$65 • 2–3 programs—$60 each

4–5 programs—$55 each • Any 6 programs—$295

Any 10 programs—$450

To order one or more of these programs, phone **800/542-4252**, visit our Web site at **www.briantracy.com**, or write to Brian Tracy International, 462 Stevens Avenue, Suite 202, Solana Beach, CA 92075. Fax: 858/481-2445.

Unconditionally guaranteed for one full year or your money back!

If you are not delighted with these learning programs, return the materials for a complete refund anytime in the year following the date of purchase.

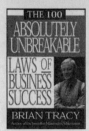

Index

A

ABCDE Method, 31–34, 90, 110
action: bias for, 103; motivating yourself into, 81–84; without planning, 14
action orientation, 3, 83, 96, 101
action taking, on plan, 10
activities: discontinuing lower value, 86; highest value, 43–44; reviewing outside, 87; reviewing work, 88
advance planning, 109
analyzing current energy levels exercise (eating the frog), 79
appointments with yourself, 98
appraisal of your work, inviting, 40
asking yourself key questions exercise (eating the frog), 60
assets, personal, 57–58
attitude toward time, 26
audio programs, 54
avoiding procrastination, 97. *See also* procrastination

B

backlogged work, 42
Banfield, Edward, 25–26
becoming a "do-it-to-yourself" project exercise (eating the frog), 55
"bias for action," 103
Brandon, Nathaniel, 72
breaking down large tasks exercise (eating the frog), 96

C

catching up, 42
Cathcart, Jim, 6
cheerleading yourself, 81–84
choke points, 62, 64–65, 111
chunks of time, creating large, 97–100, 112

clarity, 7–8, 43–44, 109. *See also* focus
"compulsion to closure," 94
Confucius, 67
consequences of tasks/activities: considering, 25–29, 110; noncompletion, 41–42; prioritizing, 32
continuous learning as minimum requirement, rule of, 52
controlling your thoughts exercise (eating the frog), 84
control of time management, 22
courses/seminars, 53
creating a "forcing system" exercise (eating the frog), 74
creative procrastination, 85–88, 112

D

daily lists, 16
daily planning, 13–17
daily review of goals, 11
deadlines, 9, 42
deciding what you want, 8–9
definitions of constraints, 64
deliberate procrastination, 87. *See also* procrastination
determination, 6
developing habits of high productivity exercise (eating the frog), 92
developing sense of urgency exercise (eating the frog), 104
developing your self-image, 6
difficult tasks, 89–92, 112
discipline. *See* self-discipline
discontinuing lower value activities, rule of, 86
discouragement, 52–53
distractions, eliminating, 98
Drucker, Peter, 43

E

earning ability, 57–58
eating the frog, origin of term, 2
Efficiency Curve, 107
80/20 Rule, 19–22, 63, 110
eliminating tasks, 33, 86
endorphins, 4
energies, focusing your, 59
energy levels, 77–78, 79, 81, 103
exercises (eating the frog): analyz-
    ing current energy levels, 79; ask-
    ing yourself key questions, 60;
becoming a "do-it-to-yourself" proj-
    ect, 55; breaking down large tasks,
    96; controlling your thoughts, 84;
creating a "forcing system," 74;
    developing habits of high produc-
    tivity, 92; developing sense of
    urgency, 104; identifying con-
    straints, 65; identifying key result
    areas, 40; laying out/organizing
    goals, 18; overcoming procrastina-
    tion, 70; practicing ABCDE
    Method, 34; prioritizing tasks, 23;
    reviewing tasks list, 29; setting
    up your work environment, 48;
    sitting and reflecting, 45; taking
    action, 108; time management,
    100; writing list of goals, 12;
    "zero-based thinking," 88

F

failure, causes of, 14, 27
"failure to execute," 3–4
fast tempo, 103
fatigue, 75–77
feedback, 40, 98
financial independence, 69
"flow," mental state of, 102
flying on business, 99
focus. *See also* clarity: on key results,
    35–40; maintaining, 43–44; and
    sense of strength, 107
forward momentum, 94
future intent, rule of, 27
future orientation, 26, 27

G

"gifts of time," 99
goals: clarity of, 7–8; getting highest
    returns, 14; steps for achieving,
    8–11; visualizing continually, 83
Goethe, Johann Wolfgang von, 44
grading your key result areas, 37

H

habits: doing your most difficult
    task first, 89–91; pressuring your-
    self, 72; setting priorities, 4; task
    completion, 5
handling tasks, 105–108, 112–113
happiness, requirements for, 75
highest value activities, 43–44
high-value tasks, 21, 102
homework, 110–111
honesty, looking at weaknesses
    with, 63
Hubbard, Elbert, 107

I

identifying constraints exercise (eat-
    ing the frog), 65
identifying key result areas exercise
    (eating the frog), 40
identifying your key constraints,
    61–65, 111

J

jobs, breaking down into key areas,
    36
job skills, 36

K

key constraints, identifying your,
    61–65, 111
key results, 35–40, 110

L

lack of ability, 52
lack of confidence, 51
large chunks of time, creating,
    97–100, 112
Law of Forced Efficiency, 41–45, 110

laying out/organizing goals exercise (eating the frog), 18
leaders, 71
learning, ongoing, 52–54
lessons, looking for valuable, 83
life management, 22
life responsibilities, 58
limiting factors, 61–65
list making: applying ABCDE Method, 32–34; to discover limiting factors, 63; increasing productivity by, 14–15; needs for goal achievement, 9–10; for next day, 90; organizing list into plan, 10
long-term thinking, rule of, 26
"long-time perspective," 25–26
low-value tasks, 21, 22, 86, 101

M
MacKenzie, Alex, 14
management, key result areas of, 36
management skills, personal, 89
master lists, 15
mental state, 102
momentum, 106
Momentum Principle of success, 103
monthly lists, 15
motivation: getting started/keeping going, 103–104; improving in skill areas, 37–38; motive as requirement for, 28; self-, 81–84, 106, 111–112; waiting for, 71

N
never having enough time, rule of, 42
nutrition, 78

O
office space, setting up your, 48
oil barrel analogy, 68, 111
optimism, 82–83
organization of daily/weekly calendar, 74
organizations, biggest problems of, 3–4

overcoming procrastination. See procrastination
overcoming procrastination exercise (eating the frog), 70
overwhelming tasks, breaking down, 93–96

P
Pareto, Vilfredo, 19
Pareto Principle, 19–22
performance: keys for high levels of, 3, 99, 101; maximizing your, 75–79; starting point for high, 37
performers, high versus low, 86
persistence, 107
personal effectiveness, 17, 43, 102
personal management, 22, 89, 113
personal powers, maximizing your, 75–79, 111
plan-making: breaking down a plan into steps, 13–17; organizing steps for goal achievement, 10
planning in advance, 109
positive addictions, developing, 4–5
positive self-talk, 82
potential consequences of doing/ not doing a task, 25–29
practice: of creative procrastination, 85–88; daily, 113; developing habit of, 5–6; as key to success, 5
practicing ABCDE Method exercise (eating the frog), 34
predictors of social/economic mobility, 25–26
preparation, 47–50, 90, 106
preplanned time slots, 98
pressuring yourself, 71–74, 111
prioritizing tasks exercise (eating the frog), 23
priority setting: ADCDE Method for, 31–34; evaluating tasks for, 28; laying out goals by, 18
procrastination: avoiding, 97; creative, 85–88, 112; least important tasks and, 20; overcoming, 39, 47, 48, 67–70, 73, 89; reasons

procrastination, *continued*
for, 7–8, 37–38, 51, 93; summary
of ways to stop, 109–113
productivity: doing your homework,
51–55; keys to high, 99, 101; maximizing your, 75–79
progress, accelerating your, 6
project tasks, organizing, 16
"Proper Prior Planning Prevents
Poor Performance" (six "P" formula), 14, 110

Q

qualities to develop for success, 5–6

R

reading, in your field, 53
reasons for procrastination. *See*
procrastination
reputation, 72, 104
resolutions, daily steps toward
goals, 10
responsibility, accepting, 84
results, focusing on key, 35–40
reviewing tasks list exercise (eating
the frog), 29
Riley, Pat, 52
rules: continuous learning as minimum requirement, 52; discontinuing lower value activities, 86;
80/20
Rule, 19–22, 63, 110; future intent,
27; key result areas, 37; long-term
thinking, 26; never having enough
time, 42; taking time off, 77; task
prioritizing, 32; 10/90 Rule, 17

S

"salami slice" method, 93
saying "no," 86
self-confidence, lack of, 51
self-discipline, 90–91, 106–107
self-esteem, 72, 82
self-image, 6, 16
sense of urgency, developing a,
101–104

sequence, laying out tasks by, 18
sequence of events, control over, 22
setting priorities, habit of, 4
setting up your work environment
exercise (eating the frog), 48
short-term pleasure versus long-
term planning, 27
single handling tasks, 105–108,
112–113
sitting and reflecting exercise (eating the frog), 45
six "P" formula ("Proper Prior Planning Prevents Poor Performance"), 14, 110
skills: asking yourself about your
most important, 39; key result
areas of, 37–38; learning new,
52–53; personal management, 89;
upgrading your, 51–52
sleep, importance of, 75–77
special talents, leveraging your,
57–60, 111
standards, setting your, 72
state of flow, 102
step-by-step activity planning, 13–17
step-by-step task completion, 94
success: determinants of, 4; developing positive addictions, 4; future orientation, 26; keys to, 59,
64, 73; Momentum Principle of,
103; optimism and, 82–83; qualities to develop for, 5–6; and self-
discipline, 107; thinking on paper,
8–11
successful people: attributes of, 3;
qualities of, 96; and time management, 97–100
superior thinkers, 25
"Swiss cheese" method of working,
94
systematic time planning, 16

T

taking action exercise (eating the
frog), 108
taking time off, 77

talents, leveraging your, 57–60,
111
task areas, key result, 36–37
task completion, 4, 5
task prioritizing, rule of, 32
tasks: breaking huge down to man-
ageable, 67–70, 93–96, 112; doing
the most difficult first, 89–92, 112;
evaluating significance of, 25; getting better at, 52; organizing, 16;
prioritizing, 21; selecting, 1–2, 90;
single handling every, 105–108,
112–113; worth of some over
others, 20
tempo, 103
10/90 Rule, 17
tension relieving versus goal achieving, 27
thinking, about task completion,
21–22
thinking on paper, 8–11, 18, 32–34
"time horizon," 26
time management: creating large
chunks of, 97–100, 112; figuring
out most valuable use of time, 44;
getting better at your key tasks,
52; as life management, 22; run-
ning out of, 41–42; wasting, 101;
wasting by stopping and starting
tasks, 106; your attitude toward,
26

time management exercise (eating
the frog), 100
time off, taking, 77
time planning, systematic, 16
tiredness, 75–77

U
unconscious procrastination, 87.
See also procrastination
unsuccessful people, 27
urgency, developing sense of,
101–104
"urge to completion," 94

V
vacations, 77

W
Waitley, Dennis, 27
wasted time, avoiding, 14
weakness, disregarding, 52
weekly lists, 15
work environment, 48, 90
work habits, 98–99
writing down goals, 9
writing list of goals exercise (eating
the frog), 12

Z
"zero-based thinking" exercise
(eating the frog), 88

About the Author

BRIAN TRACY is a professional speaker, trainer, and consultant and is the chairman of Brian Tracy International, a training and consulting company based in Solana Beach, California. He is also a self-made millionaire.

Brian learned his lessons the hard way. He left high school without graduating and worked as a laborer for several years. He washed dishes, stacked lumber, dug wells, worked in factories, and stacked hay bales on farms and ranches.

In his mid-20s, he became a salesman and began climbing up through the business world. Year by year, studying and applying every idea, method, and technique he could find, he worked his way up to become chief operating officer of a $265-million development company.

In his 30s, he enrolled at the University of Alberta and earned a bachelor of commerce degree, then he earned a master's degree in administration and management from Columbia Pacific University. Over the years, he has worked in 22 different companies and industries. In 1981, he began teaching his success principles in talks and seminars around the country. Today, his books, audio programs, and video seminars have been translated into 20 languages and are used in 38 countries.

Brian has one single focus. He believes that the average (or above-average) person has enormous un-tapped potential. He believes that you can move ahead far faster toward your goals if you learn and practice the key methods, techniques, and strategies used by other successful people who have gone be-fore you.

Brian has shared his ideas with more than two mil-lion people in 23 countries since he began speaking professionally. He has served as a consultant and trainer for more than 500 corporations. He has lived and practiced every principle in this book. He has taken himself and countless thousands of other people from frustration and underachievement to prosperity and success.

Brian Tracy calls himself an "eclectic reader." He considers himself not an academic researcher but a synthesizer of information. Each year he spends hun-dreds of hours reading a wide variety of newspapers, magazines, books, and other materials. In addition, he listens to many hours of audio programs, attends countless seminars, and watches numerous video-tapes on subjects of interest to him. Information